A Guidance Guide for Early Childhood Leaders

**Other Books by Dan Gartrell**

*A Guidance Approach for the Encouraging Classroom*

*The Power of Guidance: Teaching Social-Emotional Skills in Early Childhood Classrooms*

*Education for a Civil Society: How Guidance Teaches Young Children Democratic Life Skills*

*Guidance for Every Child: Teaching Children How to Manage Conflict*

# A Guidance Guide for Early Childhood Leaders

## Strengthening Relationships with Children, Families, and Colleagues

Dan Gartrell, EdD

Redleaf Press®
www.redleafpress.org
800-423-8309

Published by Redleaf Press
10 Yorkton Court
St. Paul, MN 55117
www.redleafpress.org

First edition 2020
Cover design by Renee Hammes
Cover illustration by AdobeStock/izumikobayashi
Interior design by Douglas Schmitz
Typeset in Utopia and Gora
Printed in the United States of America
27 26 25 24 23 22 21 20      1 2 3 4 5 6 7 8

Library of Congress Cataloging-in-Publication Data

Names: Gartrell, Daniel author.
Title: A guidance guide for early childhood leaders : strengthening
  relationships with children, families, and colleagues / Dan Gartrell.
Description: First edition. | St. Paul, MN : Redleaf Press, 2020. |
  Includes bibliographical references and index. | Summary: "In this
  follow-up to Guidance for Every Child, author Dan Gartrell expands on
  the advice broached in that book-that child need guidance rather than
  discipline. Dan gives examples of how children's mistaken behavior (not
  misbehavior) can play out in the classroom and provides strategies on
  how teachers can help"— Provided by publisher.
Identifiers: LCCN 2020005440 (print) | LCCN 2020005441 (ebook) | ISBN
  9781605546889 (paperback) | ISBN 9781605546896 (ebook)
Subjects: LCSH: School discipline--United States. | Conflict
  management--Study and teaching (Early childhood)--United States. |
  Interpersonal relations in children--United States. | Teacher-student
  relationships--United States. | Parent-teacher relationships--United
  States. | Early childhood teachers--Professional relationships--United
  States.
Classification: LCC LB3012.2 .G373 2020 (print) | LCC LB3012.2 (ebook) |
  DDC 372.21--dc23
LC record available at https://lccn.loc.gov/2020005440
LC ebook record available at https://lccn.loc.gov/2020005441

Printed on acid-free paper

*To my wife, Professor Julie Jochum.*
*Thank you, Dr. J, for your helpful input and endless support.*

# Contents

# A Readable Introduction

GUIDEBOOKS ARE TYPICALLY MATTER-OF-FACT, to the point, and semi-interesting. They provide information in a concise way but neglect, as is often done in our world, an essential understanding about learning. Every act of learning, by each of us every moment of our lives, has not just a thinking dimension but also a feeling dimension. Unless the learning act is understandable and also *feels right*, it will have limited long-term benefits for us. In 1969 psychologist and theorist Carl Rogers called positive learning that stays with us *significant learning*. Significant learning is at the heart of developmentally appropriate practice. And to encourage significant learning is why we use *guidance*.

For many years, early childhood (EC) teachers, supervisors, and trainers have encouraged me to write a book such as this. Over my fifty-year career, I have worked closely with these leaders in many settings. Regarding "a big bunch" of matters, I have listened, discussed, counseled, civilly disagreed, and supported them—always appreciating the importance of their roles and understanding how hard they work.

This guidebook is meant for people in leadership roles in EC programs, ranging from directors and principals, to classroom managers and lead teachers, to trainers and coaches, to experienced EC teachers, caregivers, home visitors, and family child care providers. Throughout the book, I refer to you as leaders (and for variety "professionals" and sometimes "teachers"—in the general sense) because leaders are what you are. Every day you are touching the lives of the children, coworkers, and families you work with. My task in writing this guidebook is to encourage you toward further engaging in significant learning about guidance.

> Who is a teacher? I like the pragmatic definition that children give: anyone in the setting who is bigger than they are. In my book—oh yeah this is my book—a teacher is an EC leader who works in a professional capacity with children, staff, and/or families in the program. In other words, administrators are teachers too. "Teacher" is meant in this general sense.

Leaders who use guidance do what very good teachers have always done, teach for meaningful emotional learning that works with, and not against, cognitive learning. If you think about it, guidance leadership pertains no less to working with staff, family members, and coworkers—as chapters 6 and 7 emphasize. This book is about using guidance in an inclusive manner with the different populations EC leaders work with.

Occasional humor is sprinkled throughout this book, ranging in quality from fairy dust to troll droppings, to keep things light-ish. Each chapter offers "balloons" to highlight key ideas. Concluding each chapter is a wrap-up section, a single take-away question that encourages readers to apply ideas from the book to their actual situations, and reference notes.

This book uses abbreviations selectively and usually for quite familiar EC terms. Some key terms and their abbreviations are early childhood (EC); prekindergarten (pre-K); kindergarten (K); developmentally appropriate practice (DAP); and National Association for the Education of Young Children (NAEYC). To me, all child care is educational for children and needs to result in significant learning every day. So the term in the book for early childhood education is ECE rather than ECCE (early childhood care and education). A few other abbreviations for guidance terms I often use appear in some chapters of the book.

At various times throughout my career, I have been a Head Start teacher, college child development associate trainer, director of a training program for nondegreed EC professionals, supervisor of pre-K and kindergarten student teachers, family child care coach, professor of EC education, and now emeritus professor of education. I have written many times on the subject of "moving beyond discipline to guidance" and still enjoy writing and speaking on this topic—so long as I can take a nap now and then! :-})

Over the years, my "output" has included the column Guidance Matters in the National Association for the Education of Young Children's journal *Young Children* and many articles in EC journals and magazines. I have also written a textbook, *A Guidance Approach for the Encouraging Classroom,* now in its sixth edition, and four other books, two published by Redleaf Press. This guidebook has connections to my earlier works and especially to *Guidance for Every Child: Teaching Young Children to Manage Conflict* (2017), also published by Redleaf Press. Where an idea in the guidebook connects with a more thorough treatment elsewhere, reference is made to the source and a link is given, often to resources on my website, www.dangartrell.net. But for all that, I have written this book to be used on its own. After all these years of writing about guidance, hopefully I have finally gotten it right. :-})

Since 1970 I have done more than three hundred trainings and presentations in most states, Germany, and Mexico. I have always tried to use some of the same guidance communication practices in my sessions that are discussed in chapter 3, a key chapter in the book. Friendly humor and receptiveness to the input of others are two. Readers who have attended any of my trainings or presentations might enjoy coming across some of the same one-liners and stories in this guidebook as they did prior. (Notice I said "might"—some of these "sharings" are on the order of old troll stools.)

Most of the references in this guidebook are to my other published works. This is not the case in the other works, but I see this guidebook as a culmination of my guidance authorship and so refer readers to my earlier writings on various topics. My apologies if the self-referencing becomes tedious.

## Thanks to the People Who Helped

Three long-time colleagues deserve my thanks: Leah Pigatti, June Reineke, and Dacia Dauner. Leah, Dacia, and June began as teachers in EC classrooms and over time became directors of their programs. Two of them were my students, and two have completed doctorates. The three together have more than eighty years of EC leadership experience and yet are all much younger than me!

In addition, Bryan G. Nelson, founding director of MenTeach, gave me helpful feedback in chapter 7 in the section on male EC teachers. These four professionals, with Professor Leah Pigatti in the lead, carefully read and gave useful feedback during this project. Over the years, Leah has been a steadfast reviewer of my manuscripts, and for this great gift, I tip my toupee! The readers made the work better.

Finally, thanks go to the entire editorial and production staff at Redleaf Press. It's nice to have a nationwide, nonprofit publisher right in the neighborhood in St. Paul. I give special thanks to editors David Heath, Douglas Schmitz, Christine Florie, and senior editor Melissa York for their patience and professional competence.

### Reference Notes

Rogers, Carl. 1969. *Freedom to Learn*. London: Pearson.

# CHAPTER 1

# Guidance: What It Is

BY BRINGING NEGATIVE ATTENTION to children when they "misbehave," conventional discipline carries the heavy baggage of punishment. We intuitively know the importance of not punishing young children. If we think about it, the children we work with are only months old. A two-year-old has less than thirty-six months of on-the-ground experience. A three-year-old only has thirty-six to forty-seven. A big, honking just-five-year-old has only sixty months, one-eighteenth of the projected life span of many young children today.

Young children are just beginning the complex emotional-social learning process that continues throughout their lives. How complex? Many of us know folks in their seventies who have a hard time expressing strong emotions in nonhurting ways. Young children are just beginning this vital lifelong learning that even senior adults have not always mastered! Being only months old, young children are going to make mistakes in their behavior, sometimes spectacularly, as all beginners do.

## Learning from Mistakes

Guidance is teaching for healthy emotional and social development. On a day-to-day basis as conflicts occur, leaders who use guidance teach children to learn from their mistakes rather than punish them for the mistakes they make. Teachers help children learn to solve their problems rather than punish children for having problems they cannot solve. In the guidance approach, leaders first assist children to gain their emotional health in order to be socially responsive and then support their social skills that are needed to build relationships and solve problems cooperatively. For this reason, in a change from my earliest works, I make a practice of referring to "emotional-social" development and not the other way 'round.

Even though it rejects punishment, guidance is authoritative ("possessing recognized or evident authority; clearly accurate or knowledgable" [Merriam-Webster 2020]). No one is to be harmed in the early childhood learning community—child or adult. But in the guidance approach, the professional is firm and friendly—not firm and harsh. There are consequences for when a young child causes a serious conflict. But the consequences are for the adult as well as the child. The adult needs to work on the relationship with the child and use communication practices that calm and teach, not punish. The consequence for the child is to learn another way.

Using conventional discipline, a teacher puts fifty-four-month-old Marcus on a time-out chair for taking a trike from Darian, a younger child. (Darian objected loudly and was forced off.) In the time-out, Marcus is *not* thinking, "I am going to be a better child because the teacher has temporarily expelled me from the group. Next time I will not take things from others. I will patiently wait my turn—and am not thinking at all about getting back at Darian!" Really, Marcus feels embarrassed, even humiliated, upset, and angry—far from the emotional set needed to figure out what happened and what would be a better response in the future. (Thought: Isn't the adult here contributing to a bully-victim dynamic?)

Whatever the noble linguistic roots of the term *discipline*, to discipline a child has come to mean "to punish." Again, *punishment makes it harder for children to learn the very emotional-social capacities we want them to learn*, such as waiting for a turn on the trike or using the trike together.

In contrast a leader who uses guidance intervenes without causing embarrassment; helps one or both children calm down; talks with the two about what happened; guides them toward another way to handle a similar conflict in the future; and facilitates (not forces) reconciliation. In the process, the leader conveys to the children that they are both worthy members of the group, they can learn a new way, and they can get along (avoiding a bully-victim dynamic).

The leader makes the time for this mediation because by modeling as well as teaching friendliness during conflict, *the whole group* is learning. Firm, friendly, and intelligent teaching is what I mean by moving past discipline to guidance—proactively teaching children that they are worthy individuals, belong in the group, and can learn to manage their strong emotions.

# Reframing the Conventional Wisdom about Discipline

In moving to guidance, the EC leader does well to look at three concepts associated with conventional discipline. The following table illustrates the reframing of discipline thinking to guidance thinking. Discussion of each idea shift follows.

## From "Discipline Thinking" to "Guidance Thinking"

| FROM | TO |
|------|-----|
| 1. Challenging children | Challenged children |
| 2. Being patient | Being understanding |
| 3. Misbehavior | Conflicts and mistaken behavior |

## 1. From "Challenging" Children to "Challenged" Children

A beautiful benefit of brain research that has been conducted over the last thirty years is that it is helping us understand the behavior of young children like never before. Years ago if a child caused frequent and extreme conflicts, the conventional wisdom was that this was a "bad kid," or at least a "challenging child with a bad home life." Those who believed in the positive potential of all children didn't have a lot more than general long-term studies to back their guidance efforts. Now, with the findings of neuroscience, there is more.

The matter comes down *not* to the character of the child—and whether the child is labeled "challenging"—but to the amount of *stress* the child is living with. At the time of birth, the brain's defense system, mediated by the amygdala, is already functioning. Generating emotional reactions to incoming perceptions, the amygdala is a key part of the limbic system, located within the temporal lobes in the lower area of the brain. If the amygdala senses a threat, it orders up stress-related hormones that slosh around in the brain (hypo-scientific term here), causing the individual to show survival behaviors for self-protection.

Human survival behaviors are well known—fighting (aggression), freezing, or fleeing. In this connection, babies who cry out of discomfort are showing the survival behavior of aggression. No matter what the circumstances, the persons present, or the time, babies are going to let the world know when they feel the stress of discomfort. And so it should be for their survival. In the context of the EC learning community, however, survival behaviors are often counterproductive. They are mistaken efforts at self-survival that other members of the community find challenging.

By around age three in the frontal lobes of the cortex in the upper brain, the child's conscious thinking and response systems have begun to develop. "Executive function" is the term for the mechanism that mediates intentional thinking and doing. Executive function integrates the processes of recall, idea formation, task persistence, and problem-solving.

In the young child, developing language and social awareness play a crucial role in the processes mediated by executive function. This understanding provides a useful explanation for why preschoolers bite less frequently than toddlers. Three-year-olds are gaining language skills and social awareness that toddlers have not yet developed. For me, two notes about executive function are essential (the first is political; skip to second note if you'd like):

1. Executive function begins to develop at around age three, but it does not reach full and mature operation until individuals are in their twenties. Think of the differences in the behaviors of teenagers and twentysomethings to nail down this understanding. In my view, this is why teens should not be able to purchase guns until they are twenty-one—the current legal age for alcohol and tobacco.

2. In young children's brains, the amygdala system is more fully formed than the executive function system. If unmanageable stress enters a child's life, amygdala functions override beginning executive functions. Being totally dependent on others for security, young children are particularly vulnerable to strong amygdala reactions and survival behaviors. Toxic (unmanageable) stress can result from a single adverse event or a series of events in a young child's life that the child perceives as threatening. Insecure relationships with primary family members are a widespread cause of this plaguing stress in young children, though not the only cause (see Gartrell, 2017).

Brain research has put a new focus on the role of stress in people's lives. The term *toxic stress* has come to explain stress that is beyond the individual's ability to manage. For me, however, this term can set off an either/or shortcut reaction in others. Either you have toxic stress or you don't. *Unmanageable stress* seems more nuanced, and I often use this term instead of *toxic stress*. Unmanageable stress refers to a level of stress that impedes healthy problem-solving and creative behavior.

Unmanageable stress begins where "healthy stress" ends. Healthy stress in young children, what I like to call "intrigue," is when amygdala and executive functions are integrated in activity around problem-solving and the resolution of cognitive dissonance (things that don't appear to fit together). For example, a child who relishes putting together a new puzzle is showing healthy stress. A child who doesn't solve the new puzzle but stacks the pieces in the middle of the board and says, "This is a castle in a lake," is also showing healthy stress—unless this child is told, "You are not doing it right." A child who can't do the puzzle and sweeps the pieces on the floor is experiencing unmanageable stress—likely *not* just in that moment.

Unmanageable stress felt at different levels results in survival behaviors shown to different degrees. Outside of the early childhood community, survival behaviors might help children in traumatic situations. Within the community, leaders who use guidance recognize that children who display especially the survival behavior of aggression are not "bad" children. They are showing mistaken survival behaviors and are really asking for help. Children show challenging survival behavior in encouraging EC communities because it is a safe place in their lives. They know they won't be punished for acting out with survival behaviors, even if the behaviors are mistaken.

Understanding the link between unmanageable stress and serious conflicts is important. As children become older, if they are not helped to manage toxic stress, the amygdala system becomes overdeveloped at the expense of underdevelopment of executive function. Think long-term learning difficulties here and chronic oversensitivity to everyday events that seem threatening. Leaders work hard with young children to build relationships that make stress manageable while brains and personalities are still "plastic" (pliant and rapidly forming). Professionals leverage their efforts at guidance leadership by working together with family members and fellow staff. They understand that challenging behaviors happen because children are challenged.

## 2. Patience or Understanding?

Nancy Weber first brought this idea to light in 1987. Her "food for thought" article in *Young Children* continues to be a topic of interest on the internet.

Weber's idea is that the importance of patience is overplayed in EC education, and the importance of understanding is underplayed. People often say to EC professionals that they "must be so patient," when they might not see themselves as

With Weber's permission, "Patience or Understanding" served as the first chapter of my 2004 book, *The Power of Guidance*. Out of respect for Weber's contribution, I paraphrase this idea shift in her terms—she said it so well.

patient at all. In making her case, Weber cites a definition of "patience," very close to that of a Microsoft search of "patience definition" today: "the capacity to withstand frustration, trouble, or suffering without getting angry or upset."

Weber's contention is that in Western culture, "patience" is often accompanied by an unintended passive-aggressive state of mind. She means that EC professionals, being human, at some point run out of patience and act out. A leader might "lose it" when any of the following occurs:

- A child acts out one too many times.
- Children "once again" show restlessness during large group.
- A parent misses a second conference and doesn't seem to care.
- A staff member repeats an inappropriate practice previously discussed with a supervisor.

The big switch is this: instead of relying on patience with the danger of its running out, EC leaders strive to understand. Patience might or might not then be a response, but holding back after reflection is a mindful choice and not a stoic reaction. The basic point of her article is that we are unlikely to run out of understanding. To illustrate, consider that an openness to understanding helps professionals be proactive so they investigate and perhaps learn one of the following:

- The child who acts out is arriving at Head Start on a middle school bus and every morning is getting teased.
- Teacher expectations at large-group time are just not developmentally appropriate for these children at this time.
- The parent is on her own, has three young children, and works long hours as a waitress. The family often crashes at Gramma's.
- The staff person is dealing with a family member at home who has a drug problem.

Even when the professional's learning is not this conclusive, the effort to understand tends to change the dynamics of conflict situations. The leader is more likely to remain engaged with people and events and not as likely to feel alienated from the situation—and lose patience.

## 3. Not Misbehavior, but Conflicts and Mistaken Behavior

If the trappings of conventional discipline rattle around in our heads, we tend to think of the conflicts that young children cause as *misbehavior*. The problem is that "misbehavior" carries the same moralistic cultural baggage as "discipline." If we interpret a conflict that a child causes as misbehavior, it is simply too easy to regard the matter in moralistic terms. Misbehavior is bad behavior, and what kind of kids show bad behavior? Kids who are bad, rowdy, wild, bullies, or from bad families (i.e., challenging). It is an easy slide to view children who misbehave as needing to be disciplined (punished). The misguided practice of "shaming children into being good" has long been debunked for not working. The punishment then has the effect of keeping stress high for the child, making emotional and social capabilities even more difficult to learn.

A widely accepted notion out there is that children act up to get attention, and that negative attention is better than no attention at all. I contend that *young children need personal affirmation, not "attention."* Due to stress and inexperience, they haven't learned to ask for affirmation in socially acceptable ways. Walking into the room, a child is not likely to say, "Teacher, I need a cuddle and being eased into things today. My family and I had a rough night." Instead, they react to their inexpressible stress by sweeping cups of juice off a tray. Why? Again, their plaguing stress causes them to act out in the EC community because it is a safe place in their lives—and they are only months old. The peril of displaying a pattern of mistaken survival behavior misinterpreted by adults is that it can cause what I call a *stress/act-out syndrome.*

Development of a stress/act-out syndrome in early childhood can cause problems for a person's entire life. The devastating cycle looks like this: Feeling unmanageable stress, young children

- act out in a mistaken effort to gain affirmation—and feel the adrenaline rush of the conflict;

- are punished—the adrenaline wears off and they feel embarrassed, upset, and angry;

- internalize negative self-messages, felt intuitively: "I am not a good kid," "They don't want me here," "This is not a good place," "I don't know what to do";

- with stress levels remaining high, and the anticipation of a new adrenaline rush, repeat the aggressive behavior.

The Centers for Disease Control and Prevention has done a great service by amplifying the concept of toxic stress through the construct of *Adverse Childhood Experiences* (ACEs). This is a term many readers are familiar with and about which the CDC says this: "Adverse Childhood Experiences (ACEs) have a tremendous impact on future violence victimization and perpetration, and lifelong health and opportunity. Working together, we can help create neighborhoods, communities, and a world in which every child can thrive" (www.cdc.gov/violenceprevention/childabuseandneglect/acestudy/index.html).

Research studies by Ladd and meta-analysis by Shonkoff (in Gartrell, 2013, 2017) indicate that young children who leave early childhood education with a developed stress/act-out syndrome have continuing difficulties in school and life. The studies show that for too many young people, the syndrome comes to a head during adolescence and continues into adulthood. The result is a lasting inability to form trust-based relationships and to resolve conflicts in nonhurting ways.

Instead of "misbehavior," I teach the concept of *conflict*. A conflict is an expressed disagreement between individuals. From the time a newborn first cries from discomfort to when a senior citizen would rather watch the falling snow than come to lunch, life is full of conflicts. Conflicts are a big part of life. Young children, new to group situations and unused to dealing with adults who are not family members, are going to have lots of stress and therefore conflicts.

EC leaders who view even spectacular disagreements as conflicts that can be resolved are in a philosophically strong position to help children engage in significant emotional and social learning.

Along with conflict, another term useful in guidance practice is "mistaken behavior." I first wrote about mistaken behavior in that same issue of *Young Children* that Nancy Weber's article appeared in. In considering likely motivations for children's conflicts, I proposed three levels of mistaken behavior, still applicable today:

1. Experimentation-level mistaken behavior: The "experiment" might be uncontrolled—a child comes to the building table, wants some parts, and takes them without asking from another child who has "lots." Or the experiment might be "controlled" (but goes wrong)—a child walks up to an EC professional and says with a smile, "Shit, teacher."

2. Socially influenced mistaken behavior: a child is influenced by important others to engage in a mistaken behavior. A sad example with an individual child: A child sees an adult give Jordan a time-out. Later, the child says to

Jordan, "Teacher doesn't like you, Jordan." Socially influenced mistaken behavior also might be the "catchy" kind that happens in groups. A child calls another child a "butthead." The word quickly becomes part of the group's vocabulary. (Time for a large-group meeting here. See chapter 4.)

3. Strong unmet-needs mistaken behavior: level 3 is the most serious mistaken behavior. Anyone (adult or child) can have a "level 3" day and find themselves in the middle of fairly dramatic potential or actual conflicts. But when these days become frequent and conflicts are atypically severe, these children are dealing with toxic stress and showing strong unmet-needs mistaken behavior.

As suggested by my graduate school mentor, Professor Steven Harlow, the three levels of mistaken behavior reflect children's relative states of mental health.

Children who show mostly level 1 mistaken behavior have stress pretty much in check. They are open to new experiences. In encountering them, being only months old, these young children make mistakes. Some pretty strong emotions can be behind experimentation mistaken behavior, but children at this level have enough mental health that before long they recover—and sometimes even self-teach other ways to handle future similar conflicts.

Children who show mostly level 2 mistaken behavior have insecurities about themselves and situations they encounter. They are working to manage their stress levels, but anxieties underlie many choices and decisions. These children look to others for leadership and tend to do what they think their leaders want—going along to get along. Their mistaken behaviors can be totally mild, for example, "Do you like this picture, Teacher?" asked *very* often, to a less innocent, joining with others to shun a child, "We are not going to play with you, Jordan." If children remain at level 2 as they grow, their main source of social influence gradually shifts from adults to peers.

Children showing a pattern of level 3 mistaken behaviors—serious and repeated—are dealing with unmanageable stress. The leader works hard to build secure relationships with these children and to empower them through *comprehensive guidance* (discussed in chapters 4 and 7) to progress toward resiliency. Children at level 3 are challenged, and adults sometimes find them the hardest to like and guide. But these kids also have the most to gain—and greatly need a secure relationship with an early childhood professional. If leaders do not give up on these kids, in my view, they are working at the highest level of guidance and are practicing *liberation teaching*. Leaders who are open to understanding the motivational sources behind mistaken behavior are mastering a central guidance tool.

In my first year of teaching, before I realized that men could teach young children, I taught sixth grade in a city in Ohio. I had just graduated from a progressive college, and you can imagine my shock when during orientation the principal began handing out paddles. I didn't take one, but I was working with big kids who were used to years of paddling as the routine form of discipline.

Despite many frustrations, there were real successes that year: Ruby, who went from a first-grade reading level to a fourth; Cynthia, who finished the sixth-grade reading text in a week and blossomed with a library-based reading program, and Hobart, just up from Appalachia, becoming friends with Dyson, whose family would not have been welcome there. Understandably, it was during that long year that I began thinking about teaching for healthy emotional and social development, and I have never stopped.

## Wrap-Up

In chapter 1 we talked about how conventional discipline too easily slides into punishment. (To "discipline" a child is to punish.) Punishment should not be used with young children because it elevates their stress levels. Conventional discipline actually makes children's desired emotional, social, and cognitive capacities more difficult for them to learn.

Young children are better thought of as months old than years old. They have limited experience, early brain development, and sometimes stressful life circumstances. As beginners at learning vital but complex life skills, young children are going to make mistakes, sometimes spectacularly. In progressing from "discipline thinking" to "guidance thinking," leaders move from the notion of

- challenging children to *challenged children*,

- being patient to *being understanding*, and

- misbehavior to conflicts and *mistaken behavior*.

In the big picture, guidance is teaching for healthy emotional and social development. (Robust cognitive development will then follow.) In a day-to-day sense, guidance teaches children to learn from their mistakes rather than punish them for the mistakes they make. When conflicts occur, guidance professionals teach children to solve their problems rather than punish children for having problems they cannot yet solve. Guidance begins with building secure relationships with children outside of conflict situations. Leaders who do not give up on a child are practicing guidance at its highest level: liberation teaching.

**Take-away question:** Thinking of children in your program, how true is it that children who seem to be showing positive emotional and social development also seem to be confident and capable learners?

## Reference Notes

Centers for Disease Control and Prevention. 2020. "Adverse Childhood Experiences (ACEs)." www.cdc.gov/violenceprevention/childabuseandneglect/acestudy/index.html.

Merriam-Webster Dictionary. 2020. Springfield, MA: Meriam-Webster.

Some materials in this chapter appeared originally in the following resources:

Gartrell, D. J. 2003. *The Power of Guidance: Teaching Social-Emotional Skills in Early Childhood Classrooms*. Boston: Cengage Learning. Special arrangement with the National Association for the Education of Young Children.

———. 2013. *Guidance for the Encouraging Classroom*. 6th ed. Boston: Cengage Learning.

———. 2017. *Guidance for Every Child: Teaching Young Children to Manage Conflict*. St. Paul, MN: Redleaf Press.

# CHAPTER 2

# The Theory Chapter

GUIDEBOOKS ARE PRACTICAL. As a rule, they don't have much theory. The reason this guidebook has a theory chapter is that I am betting you will find it useful. What am I betting? Hmmm. How about this? If I lose, I will inscribe your copy with 'most anything you'd like and sign it with my pen name, Groucho Shaboom. If I win, I'll do the same but use my real name! (Woo-hoo.)*

The theory in this chapter has appeared in my writings before and is the focus of my book *Education for a Civil Society: How Guidance Teaches Young Children Democratic Life Skills*. With all that practice, it is distilled to almost clarity here.

## Outcomes of Guidance: Five Democratic Life Skills

Today everything educational has mission statements, goals, outcomes, objectives, and so on. Stated directly, the mission statement of this book is for EC professionals to learn more about and practice guidance so that children can engage more fully in healthy emotional and social development, and, long term, so more adults can contribute in civil and creative ways to our still-developing democracy.

Contemporary guidance has outcomes, operational goals we nudge children to gain. In this book the outcomes are stated in five democratic life skills (DLS), which derive from Abraham Maslow's elegant construct of a hierarchy of needs, still in the curriculum of most ed-psych classes. Actually, the DLS owe as much to another of Maslow's concepts in the same book (1962/2008), the presence of two intertwined motivational sources for human behavior: the need for psychological safety and the need for psychological growth. In a coconut shell, we need to feel relatively secure in order to open ourselves to new experiences, to learning and

---

*Send one copy to me at 535A Laurel Ave., St. Paul, MN 55102. Include a bunch of stamps to cover return postage. Be sure to say whether you won or lost the bet and what the inscription might read. Should get it back to you in two weeks or less.

Maslow wrote, "If we wish to help humans to become more fully human, we must recognize not only that they try to realize themselves, but that they are also reluctant or afraid or unable to do so. Only by fully appreciating this dialectic between sickness and health can we help to tip the balance in favor of health" (Maslow 2008, 3e).

growing. The younger the person is, the stronger the need for security to grow psychologically. Kids who feel safe and loved move more easily toward intelligent and ethical thinking. Children who feel the plaguing stress of insecurity have great difficulty doing so.

Maslow's dual-motivations concept seems to me to have predicted the interplay of the amygdala system and executive function, prevalent in the modern brain research discussed in chapter 1. For me, this link makes Maslow's thinking sixty years ahead of its time, maybe more.

The democratic life skills make more sense when you see the list. DLS indicate the ability of the individual to

1. find acceptance as a member of the group and as a worthy individual;

2. express strong emotions in nonhurting ways;

3. solve problems creatively, by oneself and with others;

4. accept unique human qualities in others; and

5. think intelligently and ethically.

Individuals mostly need to gain DLS 1 and 2, which are safety-based skills, to work on and make progress toward the growth-based skills: DLS 3, 4, and 5. Progress on gaining the DLS is *not* sequential—first skill 1 then skill 2 then skill 3. Instead, children intuitively work on the skills in two blocks: first on the safety-based skills 1 and 2 followed by progress on the three growth-based skills 3, 4, and 5. Leaders work directly, intentionally, and usually darn hard to guide young children in gaining skills 1 and 2. They gradually shift from a coaching role to a facilitating role as children work on skills 3 and 4. With kids who show skill 5, leaders sit back in wonder, even if the children only show the skill occasionally (like many adults?).

Note that DLS theory is not about idealizing the motives and actions of children. True, children who act mostly at levels 3, 4, and 5 are a blessing. But the theory is not even remotely about turning children into "the angels they really are." The DLS are about guiding young children to manage rejection and anger and to progress toward self-acceptance, problem-solving, and perspective-taking. This progress is a lifelong undertaking, so much more possible if humans can start this essential emotional-social-cognitive process early in life.

A key objective in guidance practice is for leaders to view children at levels 1 and 2 *not* as "a pain in the backside" but as a professional challenge. Children who have difficulty meeting safety needs are worthy of secure relationships with teachers no less than children who have had an easier time with early emotional-social development. The professional challenge is worth the effort. The quality of children's lives into adulthood depends on it.

## The Term *Democratic Life Skills*

Before delving into the specifics of DLS, the term *democratic life skills* needs a brief explanation. I kid that *democratic* should always have a lowercase *d*. Certainly the term does not refer to the Democratic Party; the term is meant in the social sense way more than the political. *Democratic* in the social sense means every member of the group has a say, is a worthy member of the group, and is to be appreciated. In agreement with John Dewey, the great educational and social philosopher, I contend that society is improved when more of our social groupings are more democratic—not without leaders, of course, but who use democratic values and practices in their leadership.

In line with Dewey's thinking, though he was misunderstood on this point, *democratic* in the social sense does not imply political socialism as a form of government. A bureaucracy, elected or appointed, that makes carte blanche decisions for the masses is antithetical to the democratic society Dewey envisioned. In the broad view, an emphasis on DLS means advocating for more social democracy in more of the multitude of social groupings that form our still-developing democratic society. In the EC community, perhaps the epitome of this democracy is found in group meetings, discussed in chapter 4.

Why "life" skills? Because the DLS are vital to folks becoming healthy individuals and contributing citizens. And we work on the skills every day of our lives. The five DLS frame the life potential of human beings young and old, including staff, families, and other professionals that we share our lives with every day.

## Quick and Easy Guide to the Five Democratic Life Skills

To make things concise, below is an outline that provides the operational basics of the DLS, including typical behaviors of children working on each skill, and a quick statement of guidance practices that assist children to make progress with each skill. A thorough discussion of guidance practices that assist children in relation to the DLS forms the content of chapters 3 and 4.

## The Safety-Based Skills

**Skill 1:** Finding acceptance as a member of the group and as a worthy individual
Children working on this skill might be new to the program, perceive they are in danger of being stigmatized (excluded from the group), and/or are dealing with high stress levels (due to neurological, environmental, or a combination of reasons). They show amygdala-driven survival behaviors in mistaken efforts to protect themselves. The child may well be suffering a degree of childhood posttraumatic stress syndrome.

*Typical Child Behaviors*

- finds any break from routines, "little" tasks, and "small" frustrations stressful
- lacks trust and so may resist efforts of others to build relationships
- is easily frustrated
- often feels rejected
- loses emotional control easily
- has difficulty regaining composure
- looks on or backs away and does not willingly join in
- shows level 3 strong unmet-needs mistaken behaviors

Despite the challenges, teachers work to create relationships with children outside of conflict situations, sustain relationships during conflicts, build trust levels in the child, and help the child find a sense of belonging. Teachers use guidance practices fully and intentionally (practice liberation teaching) to assist the child to learn coping skills, develop personal resilience, and grow in social awareness.

**Skill 2:** Expressing strong emotions in nonhurting ways
Children working on this skill have progressed enough in skill 1 that they are initiating regular interactions with peers and adults. Conflicts happen because

children are just beginning to learn the skills of resolving problems with others. They are still using mistaken survival behaviors, including reactive and instrumental aggression, in the expression of strong emotions.

*Typical Child Behaviors*

- still working on abilities to share, take turns, and cooperate; has conflicts in these situations

- shows frequent, sometimes dramatic frustration and reactive aggression during conflicts

- may show instrumental aggression (like bullying) toward younger/smaller children

- quickly reacts to adult intervention with sometimes intense emotional expressions—aggression and/or psychological distancing

- able to salvage some self-esteem after guidance interventions (more so than kids at DLS 1)

Teachers use what they have learned about what works with these children to steer them around and help them resolve conflicts. These children typically experience many problems around property: "I am using this; you can't." "You put it down, so it's my turn now." Teachers use calming techniques, guidance talks, conflict mediation, and sometimes class meetings when a child experiences conflicts (see chapter 4). Importantly, leaders avoid embarrassment and shame as they sustain relationships and teach alternatives to hurting behaviors. The primary task is to be firm but friendly in teaching children to manage and use nonhurting ways of expressing their emotions.

Two notes: (1) Public embarrassment is the most prevalent form of punishment in early childhood settings. I once heard a student teacher call out the same child's name twelve times during a story. (The teacher would have been happy to sit next to the kid and help him keep focused if the student teacher had asked.)
(2) The most common sources of conflict in early childhood settings are over property, territory, and privilege. Younger children have conflicts more over property. Older children have conflicts more over privilege (Gartrell 2013).

## The Growth-Based Skills

**Skill 3:** Solving problems creatively, independently, and in cooperation with others

Children work on this skill in two dimensions: as individuals and together with others.

1. Individually, the child summons the capacity to engage, focus, persevere, and solve the activity they are working on, in the child's own way. An example is a preschooler who mixes up the pieces of five "easy" puzzles and puts them together at the same time.

2. Together with others, there is the give-and-take of cooperation in completing the task with each child engaging, focusing, persevering, and together solving the problem. An example is three kindergarten children who build a three-story "Hogwarts" with blocks, put miniature figures in "windows" on each level, and agree this is Harry, Hermione, and Ron waiting for Hagrid. The three argue about who is which figure and which figure should go in what window, but they work it all out.

*Typical Child Behaviors*

Individually:

- accesses and engages with open-ended learning activities
- perseveres with problems and tasks
- solves problems, obtains results, and creates products in their own way
- can handle failure, as long as the effort has personal meaning
- finds personal gratification in the problem-solving
- on occasion (especially if interrupted) is likely to show level 1 mistaken behaviors

In cooperation with others:

- through give-and-take, accesses and engages with open-ended learning activities
- through give-and-take, stays on problems and tasks
- through give-and-take, solves problems, obtains results, and creates products in a unique way
- through give-and-take, can handle failure somewhat, as long as the effort has personal meaning

- through give-and-take with others, finds personal gratification in the problem solving

- during the give-and-take shows some level 1 and level 2 mistaken behaviors

Teachers provide a learning environment in which children can actively engage in problem-solving—independently and in cooperation with others. They provide a variety of learning opportunities so that every child can engage in problem-solving. They recognize that the process is more important than the adult's product and do not compel predetermined crafts. (Not, "Make Frosty like this," but "Make a picture of you outside in the snow.") They give enough assistance, but only as much assistance as children need to feel ownership of the activity. Use acknowledgment and pause, give feedback, and use guiding questions and suggestions to support children in problem-solving efforts. (See chapters 3 and 4.)

**Skill 4:** Accepting the unique human qualities of others
Children work on this skill by venturing out of stereotypical peer groups in terms of initiating friendly interactions with others. Examples are an older child playing with a younger child. A girl and boy playing together. Children of different racial or linguistic characteristics playing together. Playing with a child differently abled. A "veteran" in the group playing with a new child. A "popular" child playing with a child vulnerable for stigma. A child interacting with an adult who may be new in the classroom.

*Typical Child Behaviors*

- joins groupings with children having differing human qualities

- initiates cooperative activity with children having differing human qualities

- initiates interactions with adults in the classroom who may be new

- shows inclusiveness toward children who may be vulnerable for stigma

- matter-of-factly discusses differences in human qualities, including appearances, behaviors, and viewpoints with an intent to understand, not judge

- on occasion shows level 1 mistaken behaviors

Teachers set the scene by modeling friendly relations and accepting relationships with every child in the class and with all other adults in the room. Through class meetings, EC professionals teach the importance of understanding human differences and of communicating with others in friendly ways. Teachers set up learning situations where children can have positive interactions with others different than themselves. Teachers use liberation teaching to ensure that all members of the class are accepted and appreciated. Teachers positively acknowledge inclusive pairings and groupings within the class. Teachers use appropriate private acknowledgment with individual children who show acceptance of others despite differences in viewpoints as well as differing human qualities.

**Skill 5:** Thinking intelligently and ethically

Children work on this skill in social situations when they think about the other child's needs and perspectives at least as much as their own. Examples: A child gives up a turn, like riding a trike, to a younger child. A child offers to share materials or an activity with others. After being hit or yelled at by another, a child does not retaliate but negotiates a solution. A child expresses how another child, perhaps upset, might be feeling. A child offers to help another, child or teacher, with a task. Important here is that the child does not feel pressured to show "prosocial" behavior; they choose to do so.

*Typical Child Behaviors*

- gives up turn or materials for child who "needs it more"
- comforts another child who might be sad or upset
- plays games and does activities for the common good and not one's own advantage
- offers to help another child or an adult
- expresses how another child might be feeling
- leads others in cooperative problem-solving, includes others in doing so
- makes a choice not to take advantage of situations for one's own gain
- suggests a solution to a problem that shows thought and takes others' views into consideration
- uses perspective-taking (empathy)
- likely to show level 1 mistaken behaviors

Teachers sit back and wonder at children who consistently show skill 5. In a sense, these EC professionals have already done their jobs, using guidance and liberation teaching when children were working on the earlier skills. In the immediate situation, they supportively acknowledge the behaviors they see. Privately, often later, they convey their gratitude to the child. Leaders smile a lot around kids who show DLS 5.

## The Five Skills in Real Life

Can young children really show DLS 4 and 5? Don't these skills require more executive function than young children can muster? Anyone who has worked with young children for a time has seen them, on their own, show perspective-taking and compassion. In most young children, the actions may be more intuitive than consciously reasoned through. But accepting unique human qualities and thinking intelligently and ethically are skills some young children can and do show.

**DLS 4.** In a family child care home, Jason, aged fifty-eight months, was by far the oldest and biggest child. Jason loved using the computer, which the younger children were not as interested in. Fern, the provider, made a deal with Jason. He could use the computer every day during work time on one condition: Jason needed to invite children to join him in using the computer. He was to share the computer use with them, showing them how to play games and so forth. (This was in line with Fern's thoughtful position that technology should not be an overly individual activity.)

One morning (when I was observing), thirty-eight-month-old and forty-month-old boys happened by. Jason shared in a game with each, but soon the kids left. Then, thirty-five-month-old Jodi sat down next to Jason. Jason began explaining what he was doing and offered to let her play. Jodi shook her head but watched the game that Jason continued to explain to her for almost half an hour! When Fern

In addition to *Education for a Civil Society* (Gartrell, 2012), each democratic life skill was featured in a Guidance Matters column in *Young Children*:

**Column #21.** "Democratic Life Skill One: Guiding Children to Find a Place," September 2012.

**Column #22.** "Democratic Life Skill Two: Guiding Children to Express Strong Emotions in Non-hurting Ways," March 2013.

**Column #23.** "Democratic Life Skill Three: Solving Problems Creatively—Independently and in Cooperation with Others," July 2013.

**Column #24.** "Democratic Life Skill Four: Accepting Unique Human Qualities in Others," November 2013.

**Column #25.** "Democratic Life Skill Five: Acting Intelligently and Ethically," March 2014.

The columns can be downloaded at www.dangartrell.net/columns.

announced it was time to go outside, the two stood up together and got their coats on—Jodi only reaching in height to Jason's waist!

**DLS 5, example one.** A pre-K student teacher, Sarah, used competition to motivate her children one winter day by a race down a hall and back. As she blew her whistle, the threes, fours, and fives took off—all except for Lucy, a forty-nine-month-old who would clearly rather be coloring. Sarah yelled after her, "Hurry up, Lucy. They are leaving you behind!"

Lucy, exasperated: "I'm trying."

Carter, already on his way back, took in the situation. The sixty-month-old said, "I will run with you, Lucy." He made a U-turn and slowly trotted next to Lucy, who was moving her legs as fast as she could. "You can do it. You can do it!" Carter said.

The two finished the race way after everyone else. Carter and Sarah both gave Lucy high fives. Lucy smiled. With Carter's help, she finished the race. Sarah later thanked Carter, quietly but warmly, for his generous action.

(I later encouraged Sarah to forget the racing and just have the kids run for the fun of it. She made the change, and especially Lucy seemed more relaxed about getting the exercise.)

**DLS 5, example two.** In this kindergarten class, Teacher Darcy asked Ayesha to play a math card game with Elsa. Elsa was a new student, coming from Somalia with her family. The card game used to be called War, but Darcy changed the game to Match. Each child puts down a card, the higher card takes the lower, but the cards go on a common pile. Ayesha had Elsa play the first card. Then Ayesha quickly found a card with a lower number and put it down! She counted the numbers on the cards in English with Elsa. Elsa was pleased to have helped make a big pile. When they got done with the game, Elsa asked, "Again?"

In my view, Ayesha and Carter were both showing the perspective-taking that is central to DLS 5—perceiving the situation from the other's point of view. Carter's action with Lucy was a one-time event. Teacher Sarah said Carter continued to be friendly toward all the others in the group, but Sarah did not notice a repeat of the boy's amazing example of thinking intelligently and ethically on this day with Lucy.

Kindergarten teacher Darcy had long-term hopes for Ayesha with Elsa. After Ayesha's self-initiated altruism during the card game, she continued with more friendly mentoring of her new friend, Elsa. The two did many things together that kindergarten year. And Elsa, who was big for her age and fearless, repaid Ayesha for her friendship. Was Ayesha "cheating in reverse"? Maybe once in a while, putting other people ahead of traditional rules is intelligent and ethical. What do you think?

# Wrap-Up

We work with children on gaining the five DLS in two blocks. The first two DLS are needs-based, meaning children working on skills 1 and 2 have unmet needs for security and belonging that make it difficult for them to

1. find acceptance as a member of the group and as a worthy individual, and

2. express strong emotions in nonhurting ways.

Children struggling to meet DLS 1 and 2 have unmanageable stress levels that make them sense threats easily and resort to level 3 mistaken survival behaviors. Teachers need to use guidance intentionally and comprehensively, starting with building secure relationships with these children. As trust is established, children can make progress in dealing with their plaguing stress and seeing the world as less threatening. As the children grow to see themselves as accepted and worthy, they have fewer conflicts and are better able to manage strong feelings. They are ready to progress to meeting DLS 3, 4, and 5 by

1. solving problems creatively by oneself and with others;

2. accepting unique human qualities in others; and

3. thinking intelligently and ethically.

The central guidance problem is to provide encouraging leadership with children who are challenged in terms of meeting DLS 1 and 2. As mentioned, I call the ability to guide these children toward resiliency "liberation teaching." Liberating teachers cannot accomplish this big task on their own. They need to use guidance leadership with fellow staff and parents so adults can work together to accomplish this life-changing objective (see chapters 6 and 7).

**Take-away question:** How does your new knowledge about DLS change the way you view the members of your EC learning community and your relations with them? Bonus question: Was this theory helpful?

## Reference Notes

The five DLS have appeared in my writings for many years. The most comprehensive resource is Gartrell (2012):

Gartrell, D. J. 2012. *Education for a Civil Society: How Guidance Teaches Young Children Democratic Life Skills.* Washington, DC: NAEYC.

———. 2013. *A Guidance Approach for the Encouraging Classroom.* Boston: Cengage Learning.

Maslow, Abraham. 2008. *Toward a Psychology of Being.* New York: Wiley.

# CHAPTER 3

# Guidance Communication

GUIDANCE IS ABOUT BUILDING and maintaining secure, helping relationships. Some folks, little and big, are easy to build these relationships with; others take more effort. Guidance leaders build relationships with those they like and those they are still trying to understand better. If the other person has no knowledge of which they are, the professional is succeeding at a high level in using guidance.

> Mary, a veteran Head Start teacher in Badger, Minnesota, once shared this experience. She was walking down the main street of Badger when a former student came up to her. That student, Nancy, introduced herself. She told Mary that ever since she had Mary as a teacher, Nancy wanted to be a teacher too. Nancy shared that she was now majoring in early childhood education at the University of North Dakota. The two talked for a bit, hugged, and parted. Mary was deeply touched. As she got in her car, Mary suddenly remembered Nancy and exclaimed, "That kid?!" Mary's comment to me was, "That kid drove me bonkers every day she was in my class." My comment to Mary and to you is, "But Nancy never knew."

How do we know when we have succeeded in building a secure, helping relationship? We recognize a feeling in the other person that they can approach us, share with us, and be listened to. A humungous challenge for leaders is to find the time for the individual conversations that build secure relationships. Taking a few moments to have a *contact talk* is an invaluable investment in creating a relationship. In this chapter I focus on contact talks and eight other guidance communication practices.

Readers might note that the nine practices in this chapter are general communication techniques, usable with children and adults alike. Specific communication practices with children, designed to build relationships and maintain them during conflict interventions, are what chapters 4 and 5 are about.

Actually, you probably use some or all of the nine communication practices already and perhaps know them by other names. Other names are just fine. For me, the languages of guidance, whatever they are, make its use more conscious, intentional, and reflective. From building relationships to managing conflicts, this chapter puts nine guidance communication practices in the guidance language of this old-dude professor. Chapters that follow build on the communication practices to discuss guidance leadership with children, staff, family members, and other adults.

## Nine Guidance Communication Practices

### 1. Contact Talks

Life is full of "task talk" because there are so many tasks to be done. Everything from "Get your shoes on, and we will tie them together" to "I need to meet with lead classroom staff at rest time." In contrast, contact talks are for the purpose of spending a few moments of time together (if you'd like, "being in the now together"), sharing experiences, and getting to know one another. Contact talks don't have to be long, but they do need to happen often each day.

Sylvia (forty-five months) runs up to the director on the playground.

Sʏʟᴠɪᴀ: "Me gots new sneakers, Teacher." Pulls up pants to show sneakers that (even without blinking lights) probably would glow in the dark.

Dɪʀᴇᴄᴛᴏʀ: "I bet you can run pretty fast in those tenny-runners."

Sʏʟᴠɪᴀ: "Not tenny-runners, sneakers. Watch me, Teacher!" Runs in a circle around the director and proceeds to do a quick lap of the playground. The director gives smiling child a thumbs-up, and both go on to other things.

The entire exchange took seconds, but real listening and supportive conversation were going on. Contact talks sometimes provide information that the leader can share, discreetly and supportively, with significant adults. Leaders do the sharing to further affirm relationships. For example:

> DIRECTOR: "Renaldo, Sylvia showed me how fast she can run in her new sneakers today."
>
> PARENT RENALDO: "Yeah, she doesn't even want to take them off when she goes to bed! She puts them in a special place every night."
>
> DIRECTOR, smiling: "She's quite a kid."
>
> Renaldo smiles and nods.

For each of these practices, a specific follow-up resource is listed at the end of the chapter under the reference notes. Many of the resources are Guidance Matters columns in *Young Children*, and a few are from my textbook, *A Guidance Approach for the Encouraging Classroom*.

Quick note: If you have to put off a contact talk that another initiates, please do a follow-up. You will be surprised to hear the other begin the conversation as if no time has passed. Failing to get back to the other person is a letdown and makes more difficult the trust you are trying to build.

## 2. Acknowledge and Pause

At the heart of contact talks—in fact, a great way to begin them—is using *acknowledgment and pause* (we will call it AAP), which gives the other a chance to respond.

> After a snowstorm, thirty-nine-month-old Trina covers her blue paper with white chalk. Teacher acknowledges her effort: "Trina, you are working hard on that picture, and you are really using that white chalk." Waits for child to decide what to say.
>
> TRINA: "Yep, dis is a bizzard. My mom's back there plowin', but you can't see her."
>
> TEACHER: "I bet it's a big rig."
>
> TRINA: "It's Uncle Bert's. He says she can use it 'cause she knows how."

AAP shows that the leader cares enough to pay attention. It is a sure relationship builder—and so much more authentic than adults' conventional mental shortcut, "Good job." I once heard a kindergarten child reply to this phrase, "Teacher, you say that to all the kids."

AAP is a helpful response when an adult wants to recognize someone's efforts but isn't sure what to say. Before the pause, compliment or comment on the details that you see, for example, "You are really . . ."

- working hard on that puzzle;

- using that playdough;

- bouncing that ball;

- using careful words;

- looking sad;

- playing carefully with Bruno.

Leaders use AAP to recognize actions, thoughts, and feelings. Especially when acknowledging feelings, some use the terms *reflective listening* and *active listening*. The friendly exchange that AAP kindles often grows into a contact talk. For example:

> DIRECTOR SASHA to staff member: "Maya, you look pretty tired; baby have a hard night?" Pauses. Gives staff member a concerned smile.
>
> MAYA: "Yeah she did, and Roger was up with an earache, so guess I need an extra coffee this morning."
>
> SASHA: "Maybe we can get you a break later and you can stretch out in the staff room."
>
> MAYA, smiling: "Yeah, guess it's time for me to use that sign you put up, 'On director-approved time-out.' Thanks, Sasha."

Personal note: My downfall with these talks is that I would want to tell Maya all about my toothache the previous night. My suggestion is to be selective with personal comments about yourself. Maybe save comments about your woes for a specially selected person and time—perhaps that evening (while holding a beer or a chardonnay, but maybe not both). See chapter 7 section on *venting*.

Professionals can use AAP even with those for whom language has yet to emerge. This kind of acknowledgment takes reading of the other's face during the pause and putting into words your guess about the other half of the contact talk. To a baby in warm tones, "Now that was a great burp. It almost shook the rafters! Another one! Congratulations, Abigail. I bet you are feeling better now. Are you ready for a lullaby?" Filling the air with warm words, while smiling and nodding, builds attachments and receptive vocabularies. Warm words with kids are never wasted.

With those who mainly speak other languages that you don't, the guidance leader focuses on conveying friendliness, works hard to understand the other person, and warmly affirms mutual understandings that emerge. The saying of a friend comes to mind about return visits to New York City: "Be friendly first."

## 3. Smiling and Nodding

In group situations as well as when talking with an individual, nothing conveys you are listening and understanding like smiling and nodding. (I am not talking bobblehead here; you know how to keep it natural.) Nonverbal affirmations tell the other person they are important enough for you to pay attention and that what they are saying to you is not off-putting. (If the content is close to off-putting, you can cut back on the smile, but keep up the occasional nod to show you are listening.) Nonverbal responses also serve as a reminder to you that the person's words are important to them and deserve your respect, even if you see things a different way. Nodding and smiling can make it easier to frame your response in a way that does not seem alienating to the other person. In this case, sometimes an intentional self-reference to make a subtle suggestion is helpful.

Lead teacher Annie listens with a nod and a (wee) smile to an older parent, then replies: "Yeah, my mom fed me a tablespoon of cod liver oil every morning like you give your kids. I used to drink orange juice to cut the taste, but I still can't drink OJ without tasting that fish oil. I wish they had those fish oil gummies when I was a kid!"

Teacher listens, nods, and smiles again: "Yes, you are right, kids should brush their teeth after eating those gummies, and you have to be smarter than the kids about where you store the jar. But I still shudder when I think of those morning spoonfuls!"

Personal note: In group training situations, even with very large groups, I smile and nod when participants share. A fear of public speaking is a prevalent phobia in the United States. Being accepting of the comments of participants, big or small, is a way to ease anxieties in the volunteer and in others watching how I react to the volunteer. I am grateful when folks speak up at my sessions, even when they say the same thing someone else has just said. I usually thank folks for sharing, whatever they say, adding a comment of my own in the gentlest (and most inclusive) way I can.

In my group discussions, I am trying to build group spirit—we are all in this together—rather than single out individuals as right or wrong in their comments. In my view, a happy atmosphere in a large group makes for significant learning. One other thing: When people in the audience smile and nod at me, the speaker, I am so buoyed that I try to thank them privately later. Those of you who do this for any speaker are a gift and deserve your own bobblehead!

## 4. Friendly Appropriate Touch

Friendly touch does what words cannot. Sitting on a lap—with children, not staff or parents :-}) —a hug, a pat on the shoulder, and at the least high fives and fist bumps, are organically reassuring. Along with nodding and smiling, friendly touch is vital in the caregiver's nonverbal vocabulary. We all know this about touch, but in our age of ultrasocial awareness, programs need to be transparent regarding conditions for friendly touch.

Chapter 7 offers more information about friendly touch and the realities of using it. A section focuses on men as well as women comprising the classroom staff. The chapter includes recommended topics for a *program booklet*. Program booklets for families and new staff are essential these days. Made available electronically for sure, there is still no substitute for periodically going over hard copies with new families and staff. Developmentally appropriate practice (DAP) and child-guidance practices should be included. And there should be a section on friendly touch. Referring to this section from the program booklet of a Minnesota child care center, the following illustrates guidelines a staff-team used to begin the year.

The staff knows that some children and families are uncomfortable with touch. In line with their program booklet during beginning conferences, the staff spoke with each new family about their comfort levels. Every morning when children arrived, a staff member greeted each child with the families' preferred greetings: hugs, different kinds of handshakes, high fives, fist bumps, hip bumps (adults, not too hard on this one), thumbs-up (level or down for the child), or waves and smiles.

The staff member reads children's moods through this greeting process, of course, and follows up if they sense a need. When it seemed natural, staff continued the use of the preferred methods of touch with children during the day. This program also used the same practice when they said goodbyes at night.

Busy time for staff at arrival? Yes, but the team saw this greeting routine as an investment in the child, the group, and the day. They noticed that hugs became more frequent as the year went on.

As for sitting on laps, this practice is normal for almost all young children, but maybe not so much for their families. The team talked about such matters during initial conferences with parents. They found that parents were quite willing to discuss touch matters in the conferences, and always some parents seemed relieved.

Meeting with staff at the beginning of the year to discuss touch policy is also a good idea. Make the meeting a discussion rather than a leader presentation to encourage real consensus on the practice. One approach is to get others' takes on touch guidelines in the program booklet and go from there. Leaders need to emphasize guidelines they feel strongly about. I hope this would be one: men as well as women on the staff use friendly touch. I share two stories in these guarded times.

One: A new staff member, Mari, in a West Coast child care center was a loner and different in many ways from the rest of the staff. Other staff felt Mari did not fit in. A few weeks into the program, an influential parent brought her child's comment to the director. The comment suggested possible inappropriate touch by the new provider. Another parent got involved, adding a second "report" about possible inappropriate touch. No one on the staff said much in support of Mari. She was dismissed and faced a legal investigation. Many persons familiar with the program regarded the charges as sketchy and thought they were never adequately verified.

No one should be excluded in the EC community, child or adult. With team spirit that included the new staff person, there might have been a different outcome here. This is where guidance leadership comes in.

Two: A dedicated EC special education teacher in southern Minnesota was a young man—the first to teach early childhood special education (ECSE) in that part of the state. Some parents objected to Daren teaching their young children who had special needs. Although the ECSE teacher usually had other staff in the room with him, there were times when he was alone with children. The principal had to go to bat for the new guy. The principal invited parents to visit the one-way viewing rooms of the classroom. Daren also requested and got a glass door for the room. On this basis, the parents grudgingly agreed to give Daren a chance. A month into the program, the parents were raving about their children's new teacher.

It is sad that conversation about such an essential guidance tool has to be written in this way. Perhaps in the future such cautionary notes won't be needed. But until that time, since cautionary notes about touch need to be out there, so be it. Friendly touch is worth all this and more.

## 5. Friendly Humor

John Halcrow, an old white guy colleague (with a ready smile), used to talk about the importance of friendly humor. We all know the other kind, sarcastic humor, used to keep groups and students "in their place." Sarcastic humor is punishment. An ECE student in my class, Marcella, once shared how her fourth-grade teacher made fun of her handwriting in front of the group. From that point on, Marcella would only write in tiny lettering, much to the teacher's displeasure. (Marcella said it was the first time she had talked about this experience.) In my class, for the next assignment, Marcella handed in a paper printed in an 8-point font! With a grin, she then produced a backup in 11-point font. I nodded and laughed—as opposed to when another student, Hunter, gave me an assigned three-page paper in 18-point font! (Hunter did not have a backup.) I grinned at Hunter and tried not to use a sarcastic tone when I said, "At last, a paper I can read without my glasses."

Friendly humor means finding humor *with* another person, *not* at their expense. Friendly humor assists an EC professional to build relationships, diffuse tense situations, and make it through the occasional craziness in every work setting. Friendly humor puts people at ease. For some of us, the humor comes naturally. Others have to work hard to get another to smile. The good news is that the jokes don't have to be great, just well-intended.

Teacher to boys who are quarreling: "You two sound like growling bears with stomachaches over here. Sort it out or find different lairs to work in. Which will it be?"

Leader to two new staff texting during outdoor play: "Our guideline is we stop texting when the phones get too hot or when children are present. What can you do with the kids instead?"

EC professional to parent: "Gloria, I am still smiling. During that cloudburst today, I told the kids it was raining cats and dogs out there. Louella said, 'And elephants even!' She said it better than I did!"

Besides teachers' creating friendly humor, there is the hugely important second aspect: finding humor in the amazing situations that happen every day, starting with the children themselves. An email from a teacher to her dear professor, Barb Gander, at the University of Wisconsin–La Crosse, illustrates the importance of friendly humor, starting from the usual source, "the mouths of babes." The email is used with permission.

Hi Barb!

I hope you are well! I'm now a Head Start teacher in Milwaukee, and I have a little guy in my class this year that reminded me of a story you told us in one of your classes. So I thought I would say hi and share my story.

I have a kid in my class, I'll call him JeRell, who is super impulsive and swears more than anyone I know. He's working on being kind to his peers. He likes to be a helper, so I asked him if he would hold a new friend's hand (I'll call the new friend DaShaun) to help him walk down the hallway. We have lines on the floor in my school to follow as we walk places, and everyone is supposed to follow the blue line. As I'm leading my class outside, I hear JeRell say in a fierce tone, "DaShaun! Get on the f*cking blue line! I'm not playing!" I asked him if he could say that in a nicer way and he says *in a much sweeter tone*, "Sure Ms. McE . . . DaShaun—Get on the f*cking blue line. . . . I'm not playing, ok?" And JeRell was SO proud of himself for following directions! I just kept walking and almost died of laughter—he did follow my directions :)

Nora

Often I kid about the four most-spoken languages in the United States: English, Spanish, American Sign Language, and swear words! There is no use making a federal case out of a young child's using the words he commonly hears elsewhere in his life. In talking with kids about their language, we make the point that we like how they are always learning new words and building communication skills, but these particular words bother people in the classroom.

Teaching an alternative expression like "Pickles" is sometimes a useful idea. Although, I once requested forty-nine-month-old Jerome to say "Ding-dong it" instead of "Damn it to hell." The next day Jerome got upset about something and yelled, "Ding-dong it! Damn it to hell!" I had just increased his vocabulary! (This was the story Barb shared in Nora's class.) Like Nora said, sometimes it is good to just quietly have a good laugh.

## 6. Compliment Sandwich

The compliment sandwich is a self-check on responding to others in situations that might be problematic. It is a specific nonjudgmental request for change with at least the initial and closing interactions being positive and encouraging. The purpose is to let the other know you are on the same team and not working against them.

> With child: "Charlie, you're really using that marker and making some tattoos (identified by child) on your arm. Your brother Bruce has tattoos, doesn't he? (Pause while child comments.) Well, tattoos are for some older people but not for kids, so we are going to have to get them off. I will help you with the special soap and sponge, and I bet you can get a good start by yourself. Your brother is a special guy, isn't he?"

> With staff member: "Marlo, the seven assessments are complete and written very objectively. Yay! Just need to finish the other five. I said by tonight, but tomorrow morning would be fine if that would help out. I always look forward to reading your reports."

> With parent: "Maybelline, you are here right on time to pick up Andrew. Thanks for remembering the talk we had, and we hope you keep remembering 5:30 sharp. Andrew will probably tell you about his amazing 'fun in the sun' picture. He said the blue circley mark is 'my dad swimming with his swim shorts on!'"

Compliment sandwiches are versatile. You can use them in an initial exchange or as a follow-up. It is best to use at least three pieces of bread—compliments—for each piece of liver or pickled-kale-with-pesto spread. Like contact talks, compliment sandwiches don't have to be long. Sometimes the other person wants them short too, especially when they know that you know the immediate history (as in the vignettes about Charlie, Marlo, and Maybelline above).

For both parties, keeping compliment sandwiches short tends to make them more effective.

## 7. Calming

When there is a fracas, the EC professional first triages for injury. That matter resolved, the priority of an adult under conventional discipline is to restore order, whatever it takes. Assuming the conflict involves one child asserting power over another, the conventional approach is to "comfort the victim and punish the perpetrator." The adult might think they are "fixing" the problem in this way—if at all, it is just a short-term fix.

I don't like labels, but for this paragraph only, I am going to keep the labels for the two children. Think about it: Who is the perpetrator being punished angry with? Yes, the teacher, who is way powerful, but also the victim. Because the teacher had to comfort the victim, this kid not only got the perp in trouble but is also "weak" and an easy target for getting even.

As mentioned in chapter 1, the conventional comforting-punishing approach, in my view, sets up conditions for a bully-victim dynamic, even in preschool. And bullying is the very practice the adult probably thought they were stopping by their intervention.

In the guidance approach, the EC professional *calms both children* and leads a mediation with the two (discussed in chapter 4). The mediator makes sure that the child with less power gets to have an equal say and that the child with more power learns whatever perspective-taking they can at that time, while still feeling they are an accepted part of the group. For all concerned, there is a big difference between these two strategies in tone, teachability, and the life lessons learned.

Let's talk about the difference between a *time-out* and *a cooling-down time* in this connection. If an adult removes a child to another part of the room as a consequence for something the child has done, this is the punishment usually called a time-out. Young children in time-out do not have enough executive function to figure out why they are there and what they should do next time instead. In contrast, if an adult removes a child to another part of the room to help the child calm down so they can talk about what happened, that is a *cooling-down time* and is guidance.

The leader might take a step such as offering to stay with the child to ease their stress levels. Some classrooms have a small corner area made up in a tropical island motif, where people big and small can go for a cool-down time. It is difficult to talk through a problem when the parties are still upset. Enough time for the child to actually calm down is essential—boys in particular sometimes take longer than teachers might expect. Cooling-down times help all (including the adult) to get calm so that problem-solving can happen. More on the topic of calming appears under the heading of de-escalation in chapter 4.

## 8. Describe-Express-Direct

So far as I know, the psychologist Haim Ginott first described the practice of describe-express-direct (D-E-D) in 1972. Ginott wrote a lot about what he called the *cardinal principle*. The idea is that you firmly address problematic behaviors, but you always protect the personality of the other. By extension, Ginott suggested D-E-D as what to say when a situation approaches crisis and you can't take the time to calm yourself before intervening.

Anger is the cortisol- and adrenaline-driven emotion usually behind the survival behavior of aggression. Whatever some say, I don't believe that we humans can control anger. Controlling anger is like being patient: we can do it up to the point where we lose it. Although you often hear this, for me it is a mistake to try to teach children to "regulate" their emotions. We adults can't always regulate our anger, and we have fully developed executive functions! Children don't.

Instead, it is helpful to think about *managing* the anger we feel. For children, using strong words is better than hitting; swearing in this sense is sometimes progress! The next step with months-old children is to teach them to use nonhurting words.

For adults, a way to manage the anger we feel is the practice of D-E-D. Leaders use this sequence when the issue has gone beyond the use of a compliment sandwich, though they might go back to a compliment sandwich in a follow-up. They use D-E-D to address the problem but protect the personalities involved.

**With children:**

*Describe*: "There are fish on the floor and the bowl is almost empty!" *Express*: "I am upset about this. The fish could die." *Direct*: "Quickly put cups of water in the bowl while I scoop up the fish and get them back in. We will talk about it later."

**To staff member:**

*Describe*: "A child is missing from your group. He is still on the playground behind the shed." *Express*: "Edna, I will explain my feelings about this later." *Direct*: "Please get to him and bring him in. I will stay here with the children."

**With parent:**

*Describe*: "Zena, you are late for the third time this week, and Colson had a hard day." *Direct*: "We want Colson to continue in the program, so please give me a time tomorrow when we can meet to talk about these things."

Notice in the third illustration that the EC professional did not express the anger she or he felt. The middle step in D-E-D was intended by Ginott as a way for the leader to consciously separate and express anger without complicating the actions that need to be taken. Ginott contended that using an "I" message here protects the other person by avoiding disparagement that the anger might slide into. Still, expressing anger during crisis management can intensify an already heated situation. This second step—using an "I" message—needs to be used selectively and with care.

Also notice that in all three cases the leader was setting up a follow-up in the "direct" step. Requesting a follow-up avoids leaving the other person hanging; doing the follow-up shows you mean what you say. D-E-D is not an end-all guidance method in itself. D-E-D is a way of preventing escalation during emotional conflicts so they can be resolved later when there is time and people are calmer.

A *guidance talk* is the term I use for when a leader talks with (not at) another individual to resolve a conflict. As with all guidance practices, the talks need to happen when the parties have calmed down. Guidance talks receive discussion in chapter 4.

## 9. Remembering Names, Conversations, and Promises

Remembering names is a gift that some folks are born with. If the skill is not a natural one, the EC leader needs to intentionally cultivate it. One teacher, for whom remembering names was not a gift, matched name tags to children, which they then wore as an attendance activity. After a week or two, the tags were no longer needed, and (in northern Minnesota), the teacher could tell Chris from Kris, from Kristin, from Krista, from Kristy, from Christian, from Chrissy (and Chrissy #1 from #2).

In a large program, one director had her staff wear prominent name tags to let everyone know who they were, but especially the director. Staff members smiled when the director would check out their tags surreptitiously when talking to them (an incentive for the director to learn their names). Remembering and using names tells people you think they are important enough to be individually recognized and to be seen as worthy members of the community.

Remembering conversations means a lot to people, more than one might think. When leaders can refer back to conversations, especially if not completed, it is a sign of respect for the other person. The other person will almost always remember the gist of the first talk and can continue the conversation as if there were no interruption.

"Trina, is your mom plowing the snow again today?" Trina: "No, she got Uncle Bert to do it. Mom is happy."

"Renaldo, is Sylvia still wearing those sneakers?" Renaldo: "Yeah, she was worried when she got dirt on them. But they came out of the washer clean, and we put them by the heater to dry overnight. She'll probably tell you all about it." Renaldo chuckles.

"Marlo, you got all the assessments in! Congratulations. Bet your fingers are tired from typing." Marlo: "Yeah, but not too tired to hold a beer when I got done. Don't have to do them again for another three months, right?" Director, kidding: "Yep three months. Want to start on them now?" Marlo, laughing (rolls eyes): "Maybe I'll wait a while on that."

Promises made can be a difficult matter. We make them to assure others that we are working together and that we're all on the same team to make things better. But with everything else we have to do, sometimes we forget we made the promise. Other times we might realize a promise just won't work out, and the easiest course of action is to put it out of our minds and move on. But promises, more than many things, impact our reputation and the sense of trust others put in our leadership. Promises need follow-ups.

Some promises are no-brainers: "Yeah, the riding vehicles do need their wheels oiled. I will ask Bernice to do it." Day or two later: "How are they rolling today?" When we are not sure we can deliver, a useful promise is, "I will see what I can do and get back to you." Sometimes a person might add, "But I can't make any promises," but then you already have. Later: "I talked with the director, and she said there is no easy way to lower the bulletin boards [so the kids' art will be at their height level]. She said to go ahead and tape pictures to that wall. Sometimes the kids decorate our [also high] bulletin board with my help. They like to show their parents their 'board.' Will this work for you?"

## Wrap-Up

In review for your one-hundred-item quiz on chapter 3 . . . Oh darn, I forgot to write up that quiz. Let's do reflection instead. The nine guidance communication practices are intended for use with both children and adults in order to sustain an encouraging EC learning community. Some practices, such as friendly touch, one would use differently with adults and children. Nonetheless, all nine are positive guidance practices for EC leaders to use.

The nine guidance communications practices are

1. contact talks;

2. acknowledge and pause;

3. smiling and nodding;

4. friendly appropriate touch;

5. friendly humor;

6. compliment sandwich;

7. calming;

8. describe-express-direct; and

9. remembering names, conversations, and promises.

**Take-away question:** In looking over the nine practices, what is a take-away idea for you from the three communication practices that touch you most directly?

## Reference Notes

Each of the communication practices is followed by references to "learn more about it." The Guidance Matters columns from *Young Children* can be accessed and downloaded at www.dangartrell.net.

1. Contact talks

Guidance Matters Column #3. "Boys and Men Teachers," May 2006.

Guidance Matters Column #6. "Building Relationships through Talk," September 2006.

2. Acknowledge and pause

In previous writings, I refer to the acknowledge-and-pause sequence as "giving encouragement."

Guidance Matters Column #10. "'You Really Worked Hard on Your Picture': Guiding with Encouragement," May 2007.

3. Smiling and nodding

Gartrell, Dan. 2014. *A Guidance Approach for the Encouraging Classroom.* Boston: Cengage Learning.

———. 2017. *Guidance for Every Child: Teaching Young Children to Manage Conflict.* St. Paul, MN: Redleaf Press.

4. Friendly appropriate touch

Gartrell, Dan. 2014. *A Guidance Approach for the Encouraging Classroom.* Boston: Cengage Learning.

———. 2017. *Guidance for Every Child: Teaching Young Children to Manage Conflict.* St. Paul, MN: Redleaf Press.

5. Friendly humor

Guidance Matters Column #5. "A Spoonful of Laughter," July 2006.

6. Compliment sandwich

Gartrell, Dan. 2014. *A Guidance Approach for the Encouraging Classroom*. Boston: Cengage Learning.

———. 2017. *Guidance for Every Child: Teaching Young Children to Manage Conflict*. St. Paul, MN: Redleaf Press.

7. Calming

Gartrell, Dan. 2014. *A Guidance Approach for the Encouraging Classroom*. Boston: Cengage Learning.

———. 2017. *Guidance for Every Child: Teaching Young Children to Manage Conflict*. St. Paul, MN: Redleaf Press.

8. Describe-express-direct

Ginott, H. 1972/1993. *Teacher and Child*. New York: Scribner Paper Fiction; Reissue edition, 1993.

9. Remembering names, conversations, and promises (I forget where this material came from. Oh yeah.)

Gartrell, Dan. 2014. *A Guidance Approach for the Encouraging Classroom*. Boston: Cengage Learning.

CHAPTER 4

# Guidance with Children

CHILDREN WHO SHOW LEVEL 3 strong unmet-needs mistaken behavior (the challenging stuff) are resorting to amygdala-driven survival reactions. They feel the stress of threat and lash out (in their view) to protect themselves. The aggression might be verbal and/or physical. In children physical aggression is more often associated with boys and verbal aggression with girls—though this isn't always the case. Either kind hurts, and there is to be no hurting in the EC community.

Two types of aggression are reactive and instrumental. Reactive aggression is spontaneous. It happens when a child feels threatened by the actions, and sometimes just the physical proximity, of another person. Reactive aggression becomes intensified by plaguing stress in the child's life. Reactive aggression is most common in younger preschoolers. Physical aggression declines in most children (boys and girls) as they learn the power of words. The exception is kids who are dealing with unmanageable stress. These children may get into a habit of using reactive aggression and continue with the behavior until proactively guided away from it.

Instrumental aggression is particularly challenging for EC professionals because it means the child "did it on purpose." Typically, children slide into instrumental aggression as older preschoolers when they gain the social smarts to try to manipulate situations. Sometimes the behaviors of kids who often use instrumental aggression bothers us so much that it is difficult to like them. Leaders do well to remember that these kids are still only months old and feel plaguing stress to the degree that

> Material on reactive and instrumental aggression appeared in two *Young Children* Guidance Matters columns:
> **Column #16.** "Children Who Have Serious Conflicts: Part 1 Reactive Aggression," March 2011.
> **Column #17.** "Children Who Have Serious Conflicts: Part 2 Instrumental Aggression," July 2011.

A quick reminder of the five democratic life skills might be handy here:

1. Find acceptance as a member of the group and as a worthy individual.
2. Express strong emotions in nonhurting ways.
3. Solve problems creatively, by oneself and with others.
4. Accept unique human qualities in others.
5. Think intelligently and ethically.

they need to remediate their tension with survival behaviors, even if those behaviors have been learned and are intentional.

Through secure relationships with children showing either form of aggression, leaders work to make stress manageable for the child, teach the child that aggression is not necessary, and guide the child to use nonhurting words. In the six guidance practices that follow, you will see illustrations of EC professionals addressing reactive and instrumental aggression, along with steps leaders can take to make aggression and other mistaken survival behaviors unnecessary in the encouraging EC community.

In the language of this book, the intended outcomes of the six practices is to guide children to gain democratic life skills 1 and 2 and to nudge them toward progress with skills 3, 4, and 5. An underlying premise in use of the practices is that the leader will be more effective in guiding children if they work with others, fellow staff, and families. These collaborations are the subject of chapters 6 and 7.

## Six Guidance Practices

The six key guidance practices are

1. an encouraging early childhood setting for every child;

2. whole-group meetings;

3. de-escalation: during conflicts, calm all first;

4. guidance talks;

5. conflict mediation; and

6. comprehensive guidance.

Each guidance practice starts with a vignette; a discussion that references the vignette follows.

The six guidance practices first appeared in *Childhood Exchange*, issue November/December 2015, as "Seven Guidance Practices for Children Who Show Challenging Behavior." (The seventh guidance practice, building partnerships with families, is the subject of chapter 6.) These practices, fully developed, form the chapters of *Guidance for Every Child: Teaching Young Children to Manage Conflict*, my 2017 Redleaf book.

As in prior vignettes, these contain a few common speech patterns of young children.

## 1. An Encouraging Early Childhood Setting for Every Child

A preschool class is walking back from the park a few blocks from the center. Just after turning a corner, student teacher Ginny kneels down to help Melissa retie her shoe. They get back to the line and Ginny notices Roger and Dennis are missing. Ginny signals to Teacher Viola, who rolls her eyes and mouths, "Those two." Ginny nods and goes back around the corner. Dennis is walking in circles, and he is bent over! Roger is sitting on a stoop watching Dennis.

Ginny approaches Dennis and gets down on her knees with her hands gently placed on Dennis's shoulders: "Dennis, the group has gone around the corner already. We need to catch up."

Dennis: "I'm watchin' the ant. It's right there!"

Ginny looks down and sees an ant approaching her left knee. "Yes, I see the ant. We will look for more ants on the playground, I promise. But right now we have to catch up." She smiles at Dennis, who reluctantly takes her hand. As they pass Roger, Ginny puts out her other hand and Roger takes it. The three hustle and catch up with the group.

Teacher Viola later tells Ginny, "I've got a great group except for those two. Dennis has no sense of what it means to be in preschool. And the way Roger always hangs back on everything, he is just not ready for our group." Ginny waits a bit before rolling her own eyes. After reinforcing the need for confidentiality, we talked about Viola's reaction in our seminar.

Some teachers would like to think that if most children in their groups are getting along and not having problems, then the program must be developmentally appropriate. Adults often rationalize this idea by concluding that the few who don't fit in are "not right" or "not ready" for the program.

It is difficult for adults to recognize that for reasons of development, temperament, gender, and/or behavior, some children just rub them the wrong way. The reality is that adults can have personality conflicts even with preschoolers! Contrary to the conventional wisdom, EC professionals need not love every child. But they do need to form a positive relationship with every child—for the good of the children themselves, the rest of the group, and the adults involved with the program. The leader uses two fundamental practices to enable every child to feel welcomed and valued.

First, the ECE professional monitors and modifies the program to make sure it is developmentally appropriate for every child. Often young children are just too energetic for a traditional preschool day that has teacher-directed large groups, follow-directions craft activities (instead of open-ended art), limited choices in the use of materials and centers, and sit-down pencil-and-paper lessons. When teachers modify the program to include many open-ended, hands-on activity choices, stable small groups that do things together, and a "big bunch" of active play experiences—outdoors and in activity rooms—more children are likely to get engaged and feel included.

Second, the professional uses relationship-building techniques like acknowledgment and pause (AAP) and contact talks. She or he looks for opportunities to spend quality time, even if brief, especially with children who are difficult to understand. Discovering what these children take an interest in, such as ants, the leader can freshen up the curriculum to bring the children, the interest, and the program together. By adding an ant farm, fiction and nonfiction picture books about ants, ant-related creative activities, outdoor science expeditions, and ant-observing gear like magnifying glasses—along with related contact talks—the leader expands the number of children for whom this program is developmentally appropriate.

Along these lines, how do you know when an activity is developmentally appropriate for a child? The cosmic response is this: when the stars of child interest, an engaging activity, opportunity for full engagement, and teacher encouragement are all aligned. The down-to-earth response is when the child's attention span for the activity is longer than yours—such as when a kid wants you to sing the book *The Ants Go Marching* for a second or third time! Every child having significant developmentally appropriate learning experiences every day is the goal.

## 2. Whole-Group Meetings

Teachers Annette and Sylvia wanted to give their space a more active option during the winter months. The two put up a four-sided climber. Even though Sylvia stationed herself close, Henrico got his fingers stepped on going up the ladder, Rorey got bumped while on top, and Dylan and June-bug collided halfway up and halfway down the slide.

The EC professionals put a "Closed until tomorrow" sign on the climber and explained the situation. The next day before choice time, the teachers called a full-group (class) meeting.

The children had already learned the guidelines for these meetings: (a) one person speaks at a time; (b) everyone listens to who is speaking; (c) be careful with names so no one is embarrassed; (d) group meetings are to make things better.

ANNETTE: We had some problems on the new climber yesterday. Can someone share what happened to them?

HENRICO: Somebody stepped on my fingers when I was goin' up!

ROREY: Some damned person bumped me on top.

ANNETTE: Can you say that differently, Rorey?

ROREY: Somebody bumped me, and I nearly felled off.

JUNE-BUG: Gees, I was goin' down and someone came up, and we crashed.

DYLAN: Well, you can go up a slide too.

ANNETTE: Well, let's talk about these things. How can we use the climber so it is fun but safe?

The leaders pause and let the children come up with ideas. Annette works with the children to get the ideas stated positively as guidelines. As they agreed, Sylvia wrote the guidelines on a chart and read them back. They decided on four:

- Give kids room when they are climbing up.

- Be careful on top so no one falls.

- Sit, scoot, or crawl on top. Don't stand up.

There was a lot of discussion about the slide. They decided:

- We go down the slide except on Fridays.

The teachers were especially pleased with the last guideline. The children would be getting extra upper-body exercise on Fridays. And the guideline provided a functional calendar activity. They all went over the guidelines during the next morning meeting (a functional early reading activity). Sylvia posted the list by the climber and after a day or two no longer had to monitor climber play close up.

The children in this situation were showing level 1 mistaken behavior. They were experimenting with a new piece of equipment, and a few of their experiments, innocently enough, got out of control.

Whole-group meetings begin where circle times leave off, going beyond the routines of weather and weekly calendar. Large-group meetings bring the events of the day, along with problems, experiences, and activity planning, into thoughtful discussion. They involve respectful talking and listening that encourages the group to share and solve problems together.

Early childhood professionals might introduce an activity: "Today in the art area, you are going to make your own special outdoor pictures. Who can think of something you like to do outdoors?"

Or the teacher might lead a discussion on a problem in the classroom that has "gone public." Play on a new climber is one example. Another is: "Yesterday, a few children were saying some words that bother children and teachers. The words were 'poopy butt' [pauses for giggles]. Could someone share how you would feel if someone says that to you?" The adult then guides the group in civil discussion about how this problem can be solved. Going along with an established guideline, the names of individual children are not used. The teacher follows up privately with children she or he knows have been using the words.

When children join together to use unfriendly words—butthead, poopy butt—they are engaging in a level 2 socially influenced mistaken behavior. Using a group meeting to discuss the problem takes away the in-group–out-group motive for using the expression. Leaders raise the matter to a full community concern: we treat each other in friendly ways. The social pressure of the community reminds children that all are worthy members of the group.

Large-group meetings do much to build encouraging EC settings. Leaders teach how they go by using them as a self-teaching practice at the beginning of the year. An effective early topic is to set up three or four positively stated guidelines that teachers put on charts and teach when children forget. An example is "Friendly touches only." Listed at the end of the chapter, Guidance Matters Columns #7 and #19 both discuss whole-group meetings further and provide helpful resources for additional exploration. So do my 2013 and 2017 books.

Group meetings are versatile in that they can address both everyday matters and public problems within the group. In response to a question that EC folks sometimes have, I know of even toddler settings where the adults hold group meetings every day. They use the clump technique with toddlers sitting on adults' laps, sensitively interpret what the group might be feeling, and keep the meetings simple and to the point. In my view, full-group meetings with any age level are a valuable lead-up activity for living in a democracy—at this level with the teacher as leader.

Further note: Consider the conventional discipline equivalent for addressing problems—the notorious group punishment. What if Annette and Sylvia had taken down the climber, even temporarily? The children would have concluded they were not worthy of using the climber; they would have been bothered at the teachers for coming down on all of them for the mistakes of a few; they would have been upset with the children who caused the group punishment; they would have been deprived of the physical exercise the climber provided. Instead, the group meeting empowered the children to be participating citizens, solving a real problem together. Group meetings take a while to become a natural part of the program. The effort is worth it. They build group spirit among all members of the early childhood community like nothing else.

## 3. De-escalation: During Conflicts, Calm All First

Benji, a child slow in his development, was playing "family" with two older preschoolers, Marlys and Stephen. They were "eating" packing beads cereal from small bowls that Marlys served from a large bowl. Benji said, "More please," but Marlys shook her head and said, "It's time to go to school." Benji got upset, swept the bowls off the table, crawled under it, and yowled. Teacher Alicia saw what happened, got under the table, and put her arm around Benji.

Benji stopped yowling but whimpered and was breathing rapidly. Alicia got him to slow down his breathing through taking deep breaths. She quietly told Benji he must have been very upset and paused. Benji said, "Marlys wouldn't give me more.

Alicia said softly, "And that made you upset." "Mad," said Benji. Stephen and Marlys stood off to the side and watched Benji and their teacher. After a few minutes, the two came out from under the table and began to put the beads in the big bowl. Stephen and Marlys helped. The three finished breakfast, then got on the bench with a steering wheel and took the bus to school.

A more technical term for calming folks down is *de-escalation*. The definition of de-escalation is "reduction of the intensity of a conflict or potentially violent situation." This more technical term sounds, well, more technical. For me, "calming all down" fits better the atmosphere and tone of early childhood education. I use "de-escalation" here so readers know I know the more technical term. :-})

In the anecdote, Benji was probably showing level 3 unmet-needs mistaken behavior. Alicia knew that Benji was subject to frequent bouts of reactive aggression. Benji was dealing with the neurological and environmental stressors that often accompany atypically developing brains.

Calming techniques received an introduction under guidance communication practices in the previous chapter. Calming is so basic to guidance that I want to continue the discussion here. Traditionally, teacher-technicians react to dramatic conflicts by quickly "restoring order." In contrast, adults who use guidance calm all involved, beginning with themselves. If children are upset, the ECE professional may remove one or both from the situation. Yet, as mentioned in chapter 3, this action is different than giving a time-out, expelling a child to a chair as a consequence of something the child has done. No one can resolve a conflict when emotions are high. A teacher removes children only to help them calm down. When calm, the teacher uses a guidance talk or conflict mediation (to follow) to model and teach problem-solving, reconciliation, and nonhurting responses for the next time there is a conflict.

Often separation to cool down is not needed. The teacher might have the children take deep breaths and otherwise ensure they are calm before helping them mediate the situation. If a child has totally lost it and there is an imminent danger of harm, the adult may need to use the de-escalation technique of last resort, the passive bear hug (PBH).

Programs need to have written policies regarding this measure—such as another adult being present and written reports being filed—before PBH is used. The measure is arms around arms, feet around feet with the child facing away from the teacher. Child and teacher go into a sitting position with the child's head out to the side to prevent head butting. The teacher may sing or whisper or simply hold the child to assist with the calming process.

At first the child feels real threat and reacts accordingly—this is not a fun technique for anyone. A general finding of folks who have had to use the technique is that the child gradually realizes the adult is there to help and snuggles in. Usually, when PBH is used, leaders need to follow up with comprehensive guidance (discussion to follow) to help the child reduce the need for repeat tantrums.

After a serious conflict occurs, think about the difference between restoring order and calming everyone down. Young children are at the peak of their learning years. This is the optimum time to guide children to learn from their mistakes. While it is true that leaders mostly build relationships with children outside of conflict situations, they work hard to sustain relationships during even serious conflicts. In the early childhood community, the leader builds this confidence one child at a time, as Alicia did with Benji.

## 4. Guidance Talks

In an older building, the children in this preschool take turns holding open the door to the outside play area for the group. Leader Kiko has a list of the children's names on a magnetic board, and the marker today is by Jayden's name. Jayden (fifty-six months) is having a good time holding the door and for fun begins swinging it toward the children as they come out. Jayden's hand slips, and the door bumps Owen hard. Owen falls down and yells at Jayden. As the rest of the children squeeze between Owen and the door, Jayden retreats back into the room.

Teacher Kiko notices the commotion and goes back to the doorway. Sitting down, he comforts Owen and hears his side of what happened. Owen then joins the others in the play yard. The other teacher stays outside with the children as Kiko goes into the room. He finds Jayden crouching behind the bookshelf in the library center.

Kiko: Jayden, I see tears on your face, and you look pretty sad.

Jayden: I didn't mean to!

Kiko: Let's cool down a bit, and then we'll talk. How about taking some deep breaths with me?

Jayden: No!

Kiko: Okay, but I will. Sometimes I forget to breath out and my cheeks look like balloons. (On the third breath in, Kiko makes his cheeks big. Jayden smiles. The kid relaxes despite himself.) So what happened?

Jayden: I was holdin' the door. It slipped and hit Owen.

Kiko: Some of the kids said there was some door swinging?

Jayden: Just a little to make them hurry.

Kiko: What can you do next time so no one gets hurt? (Pause)

Jayden: Not swing the door. Not let go?

Kiko: Right-on ideas. And how can you help Owen feel better?

Jayden: Say I'm sorry.

Kiko: All right, but he was pretty upset, so if you say it, mean it. (Jayden nods his head.)

KIKO: Now when we go in today, do you want me to hold the door so the kids know it's okay, or do you want to hold the door with me?

JAYDEN thinks about the options: With you.

KIKO: Sounds like a plan. And what are the things you are going to remember?

JAYDEN: Hold on and no swingin'.

KIKO: You got it. (Looks at his watch as he gives Jayden a friendly fist bump.)

It seemed longer, but the guidance talk took only four minutes. The two walk out onto the playground together.

JAYDEN showed level 1 experimentation mistaken behavior here, and Kiko, using a guidance talk, resolved the situation in a way that kept Jayden's spirit intact.

A guidance talk (GT) is the intervention of choice when one child gets into a conflict with a peer or an adult. As with class meetings and conflict mediation, the purpose of GT is to resolve the conflict peaceably and teach the child what she or he can learn at the time about nonhurting responses during conflicts. A primary consideration is to avoid embarrassment of the child, which is the most common form of punishment used in EC settings.

The adult first gets calm and helps the child to cool down, sometimes by moving to a quieter place in the room. Alone in the room, Kiko did not have to worry about keeping things private with Jayden. The adult works out with the child what happened, giving respect to the child's viewpoint. They then discuss how they can make the situation better and what the child could do next time instead of showing aggression. Note that the adult does not force an apology. He asks how the child can help the other person feel better. If needed, give the child time to think of a way, and for the children to get together again. GTs enable teaching for healthy emotional and social development. Kiko certainly worked toward this goal in his guidance talk with Jayden.

## 5. Conflict Mediation

Mattie and Lynda are pretty close friends, and Kayla is sometimes included in the two girls' play. This morning Mattie and Lynda are building with plastic tracks and wooden trains. They are setting the track up to drive their two favorite Thomas the Tank Engine locomotives: Emily and Mavis. Kayla comes over to join them, but Mattie tells her to go away.

KAYLA: I want to play too.

MATTIE: There are just two girl engines, so you can't be one. Go away.

LYNDA: Yeah!

Making an angry face, Kayla takes two tracks and beats hard on a box edge. Teacher Jan comes over. She sits down in between the children.

JAN (level voice): I am hearing unhappy noises. Sounds like a problem over here. (Pauses.)

Mattie and Lynda begin to explain. Kayla starts talking over them.

JAN: We will talk and listen about this, but first we need to get calm. Deep breaths please. (Lynda and Kayla take deep breaths along with Jan.)

MATTIE: I'm not.

JAN: Mattie, if you are ready to talk and listen now, that is fine. We three are almost ready. (They take a few more deep breaths.) You know how talk and listen works. Kayla talks first, then Lynda, then Mattie. Please listen carefully to the others. Kayla, what did you think happened?

KAYLA: I wanted to play with them, and they wouldn't let me. I asked nice. (Not a happy expression on Kayla's face.)

JAN: Thank you for sharing, Kayla. Anything else? (Kayla shakes her head.) Now let's hear from Lynda.

LYNDA: There was only two girl trains, and the track was for them. So Kayla couldn't play.

JAN: Thank you, Lynda. Anything more you'd like to add?

LYNDA: Ask Mattie, Jan.

JAN: How did you see things, Mattie?

MATTIE: Kayla always wants to play, but there were only two girl trains, so she couldn't.

JAN: Anything else?

MATTIE: She could play someplace else.

JAN: Let's see if I have this right. Kayla, you wanted to help set up the tracks and play trains with Mattie and Lynda. (Kayla nods.) Mattie and Lynda, you didn't want Kayla to play because you were using the Emily and Mavis engines, and there weren't any more "girl trains."

(All three girls nod.)

Jan: Well, our guideline [taught in group meetings] is "You can't say you can't play," so how can we fix this? (Pause.)

Mattie: Kayla could take some track and build over there. (Points to a spot on other side of train box about three feet away.)

Lynda: Yeah, she could use Thomas the Tank Engine.

Kayla: I want to build with them.

Jan: Suppose, Kayla, you start building over there. Could you three figure out a way to join the tracks?

Lynda: (Looks at Mattie.) We could do that? (Mattie nods.)

Kayla: I am going to build to the train house so the trains could go there.

Jan: Okay, girls, I need to know. Will this take care of the problem?

Quick nods and the three get to work. Soon the two-track lines are joined up, and the three engines are chugging—well, not Mavis. She's a diesel, so she is humming. Jan compliments, "You three are really playing together."

Afterword, Jan has a quiet GT with Mattie and Lynda about letting other children join their play. Jan also makes a mental note about structuring small groups so that Lynda has more experiences with other children.

Jan knows that Mattie tends to be the leader in these situations, and has a quiet guidance talk with her later about letting other children join when Mattie and Lynda are playing together. Mattie and Kayla were both showing level 1 experimentation mistaken behavior. Lynda, often looking to her friend for direction, was showing level 2 socially influenced mistaken behavior.

Jan could take time to mediate the conflict here because the children were engaged in various self-selected work-time activities. Developmentally appropriate work times like this foster full engagement by children. With experience at work times, children have relatively few strong conflicts. When children do, they want to work with the leader to resolve the problem so they can get back to their significant learning. If there is no time for full mediation, the teacher calms whoever is upset and sets up a time later to mediate the matter with the children. If the matter is "settled," the leader still meets with the children to go over what they can do instead next time.

Early childhood professionals use conflict mediation when two or three children experience a conflict. In Guidance Matters Column #2, "Jeremiah," a five-year-old, mediates between a thirty-month-old who has a truck and a fifty-month-old who wants it. (The younger child gets to keep the truck.) The point is you don't need a master's degree to use mediation. I write about a five-step practice, the "five-finger formula," for using conflict mediation. We use Jan's mediation to illustrate the steps.

Thumb: Cool everyone down, starting with yourself. Only continue when all are calm enough to talk.

JAN (level voice): I am hearing unhappy noises. Sounds like a problem over here.

(Mattie and Lynda start to explain. Kayla starts talking over them.)

JAN: We will talk and listen about this, but first we need to get calm. Deep breaths please. (Lynda and Kayla take deep breaths along with Jan.)

MATTIE: I'm not.

JAN: Mattie, if you are ready to talk and listen now, that is fine. We three are almost ready. (They take a few more deep breaths.)


Pointer finger: Use negotiation to get the children to agree how each saw the conflict. Be neutral and nonjudgmental about the children's perceptions; your authority comes from being the mediator, not from being an evaluative judge.

JAN: You know how talk and listen works. Kayla talks first, then Lynda, then Mattie. Please listen carefully to the others. Kayla, what did you think happened?

KAYLA: I wanted to play with them, and they wouldn't let me. I asked nice. (Not a happy expression on Kayla's face.)

JAN: Thank you for sharing, Kayla. Anything else? (Kayla shakes her head.) Now let's hear from Lynda.

LYNDA: There was only two girl trains, and the track was for them. So Kayla couldn't play.

JAN: Thank you, Lynda. Anything more you'd like to add?

LYNDA: Ask Mattie, Jan.

JAN: How did you see things, Mattie?

MATTIE: Kayla always wants to play, but there were only two girl trains, so she couldn't.

JAN: Anything else?

MATTIE: She could play someplace else.

JAN: Let's see if I have this right. Kayla, you wanted to help set up the tracks and play trains with Mattie and Lynda. (Kayla nods.) Mattie and Lynda, you didn't want Kayla to play because you were using the Emily and Mavis engines, and there weren't any more "girl trains." (All three girls nod.)

Middle finger (be careful with this one): Help the children brainstorm solutions to the conflict. If they need help with language or ideas, offer them and work for agreement. Defer to compromise solutions the kids come up with even if it is not what you had in mind.

JAN: Well, our guideline [taught in group meetings] is "You can't say you can't play," so how can be fix this? (Pause.)

MATTIE: Kayla could take some track and build over there. (Points to a spot on other side of train box about three feet away.)

LYNDA: Yeah, she could use Thomas the Tank Engine.

KAYLA: I want to build with them.

JAN: Suppose, Kayla, you start building over there. Could you three figure out a way to join the tracks?

Ring finger: Agree on a solution and try it. Use only as much leadership as you need to in order to get the children to enact the solution. Sometimes steps 3 and 4 blend together. This is fine.

JAN: Suppose, Kayla, you start building over there. Could you three figure out a way to join the tracks?

LYNDA: (Looks at Mattie.) We could do that? (Mattie nods.)

KAYLA: I am going to build to the train house so the trains could go there.

JAN: Okay, girls, I need to know. Will this take care of the problem? (Quick nods and the three get to work.)

Pinky: Monitor and follow up. Compliment the children on coming to a solution. Hold a private GT with one or all of the children if you feel they have more learning to do.

Soon the two-track lines are joined up, and the three engines are chugging—well, not Mavis. She's a diesel, so she is humming. Jan compliments, "You are really working together."

Afterword, Jan has a quiet GT with Mattie and Lynda about letting other children join their play. Jan also makes a mental note about structuring small groups so that Lynda has more experiences with other children.

Similar to the GT vignette above, this conflict mediation took only a few minutes. Does this seem like ages in the early childhood day? Maybe. But leaders take the time because of all the emotional and social development—along with problem-solving and communication skills—that the children in the conflict are gaining. As well, through observation, the rest of the community is learning that humans can resolve conflicts peaceably. Besides, solving the problem the first time reduces the chance of later flareups and the interventions necessary to resolve them.

The key point concerning mediation always comes down to this: conflict mediation does not have to be perfect but works well enough so long as the adult shows leadership by being a firm but friendly mediator instead of a police officer or an evaluative judge.

## 6. Comprehensive Guidance

Harrison was twenty-seven months old when he joined the toddler room. After a few days, he began to have conflicts just after arriving in the morning. He would not wash his hands or come to the breakfast table. When Teacher Rena tried to invite him, he worked himself into a rage, yelling the *F* word (with his own particular pronunciation) and throwing things. Because his behavior distressed the other toddlers, Rena had to physically move him to a far corner of the room and hold him until he calmed down. (She used the passive bear hug.)

When Harrison repeated this behavior over the following days, Rena talked with Veda, his young mom, whom she had met only a few days earlier. Rena said she enjoyed having Harrison in her group. But she told Veda he was having a problem, especially after he arrived, and she wanted to help him. Veda shared that their house was small, and the activities of some family members often kept Harrison from settling down and getting to sleep. From their conversation, Rena concluded that the toddler's aggressive behavior was due to lack of sleep and conditions at home.

Rena worked out a strategy with Veda and the other staff. When Harrison arrived in the morning, she approached him in a low-key way and gave him the choice of getting ready for breakfast or snuggling. Harrison usually chose snuggling and occasionally fell asleep. During the day, Rena gave him choices between two activities. Harrison began making choices and participating more. Rena and the two assistant teachers also sought out opportunities for one-on-one snuggling and contact talks—a few minutes of shared quality time—with him throughout each day.

Over that first month, Rena developed a relationship with Veda, who disclosed a bit more about the family's home situation. Rena learned that two male members of the family were particularly affected by poverty and clinical depression. This led Rena to refer the family to Early Head Start. However, there was a waiting list and therefore no opening for Harrison.

Sometimes Harrison ate breakfast. He tended to eat late and not much of what was offered, but at least he started eating. Gradually Harrison accepted the toddler routine. Rena remained open to his need for a morning snuggle, but Harrison needed closeness on arrival only some days. The staff realized that while they could not change Harrison's home environment, they could help him feel safe and welcome in the toddler room and maintain a positive relationship with his mother.

This anecdote first appeared in Guidance Matters Column #18, "Aggression the Prequel: Preventing the Need," November 2011. Used with permission from NAEYC.

When children cause conflicts that are serious and repeated, EC professionals need to bring a mix of guidance practices together in a coordinated plan. The EC professional holds a meeting with all staff who work with the child. Without being a gripe session, the team tries to understand the child's pattern of behavior. The lead adult then contacts family members, using the urgency of the situation to request a meeting.

Starting with positives about the child, the lead adult presents the problem the child is having in the context of overall progress the staff sees. The staff and parents discuss the need for a formal or informal Individual Guidance Plan (IGP) for improvement in the one area identified. They work out a plan together with the family members. The staff gives encouragement to the family to work on the plan at home. The staff monitors progress in relation to the plan in the classroom and holds one or more follow-up meetings with the parents.

An IGP planning sheet and form are available for download at www.dangartrell.net/presentation-handouts. More on comprehensive guidance and use of the Individual Guidance Plan can be found in Gartrell (2013).

Too many early childhood programs across the United States have a history of pushing out children who show serious and repeated conflicts. In the guidance approach, removing children as a result of their behavior is a last resort, only after an IGP is developed, tried, modified, and tried again. Building relationships with parents immediately is essential should an IGP later prove necessary. In making the case that an IGP meeting is necessary, staff may have to say this is the only way the child can continue in the program—though this step is not always possible. And establishing positive relations from the beginning hopefully makes this move unnecessary.

The more serious the situation, the more the EC professional involves and collaborates with other adults in finding solutions. Good relationships among adult professionals are as important as good relationships with children and families. Friendly communication is always at the heart of guidance. Rena, leading her staff, took the time and effort with Harrison and his mother, Veda. There was no magic answer here, but Rena made the EC community better by her leadership. The team used an IGP informally but effectively in this situation.

# Wrap-Up

In this chapter we looked at two types of aggression, reactive and instrumental. Reactive aggression is impulsive. A child with plaguing stress due to adverse experiences acts out using mistaken behavior in an impulsive effort at self-protection. Instrumental aggression shows intent and is therefore especially challenging for leaders. It is typically older preschoolers who show instrumental aggression. They are acting from the same motivation of high stress and perceived threat, but these kids have the cognitive development to devise strategies to assert their will in the mistaken effort to protect themselves.

We examined six ideas, key in the use of guidance:

1. an encouraging early childhood setting for every child

2. whole-group meetings

3. de-escalation: during conflicts, calm all first

4. guidance talks

5. conflict management

6. comprehensive guidance

**Take-away question:** Looking at the six guidance practices, what are your thoughts about how you might further implement three that are most significant to you?

## Reference Notes

Gartrell, Dan. 2013. *A Guidance Approach for the Encouraging Classroom*. Boston: Cengage Learning.

In addition to the Guidance Matters columns listed in this chapter, I suggest the following, which dovetail well with the chapter—classics but still worth reading.

Column #2. "Jeremiah," January 2006.

Column #3. "A Student Teacher Uses Conflict Mediation," March 2006.

Column #7. "The Beauty of Class Meetings," November 2006.

Column #9. "Competition: What Part in Our Programs?" March 2007.

Column #14. "Promote Physical Activity: It's Proactive Guidance," March 2008.

Column #19. "From Rules to Guidelines: Moving to the Positive," November 2011.

For further information on preventing expulsions in preschool, refer to Alissa Mwenelupembe, "What You Can Do to Prevent Preschool Expulsion," *Teaching Young Children*, February/March 2020.

# CHAPTER 5

# Readiness: Not a State of Knowledge but a State of Mind

WHY WOULD THAT OLD-DUDE PROFESSOR put a chapter on readiness in a guidance book? Good question. The answer is not that I had this material handy—an article of mine—and wanted to use it as filler. Well, I did have it handy, but that is not the reason the article is here. In old-dude-professor lingo, here is the answer: readiness, developmentally appropriate practice (DAP), and guidance are interconnected. Let me explain.

Guidance is organic to DAP. By now I am hoping you agree that guidance is the dimension of DAP that addresses healthy emotional and social development.

Developmentally appropriate practice is about self-selected, self-directed learning experiences accomplished on one's own and as a cooperative member of a learning community. DAP is fully working when the child comes away from an experience with a gain in personal understanding. *Significant* learning is what Rogers (1969) called it (in the introduction no less than here), learning that stays with and changes a person. A child's gain in understanding via a learning experience means that at that moment intrinsic motivation is bolstered, executive function perks along, and brains are building themselves.

An example is Shawn, a sixty-two-month-old who colors a multicolored sky because "the sky isn't just blue, you know." Especially if an adult affirms and further encourages Shawn's insight, the experience constitutes significant learning for the child—and perhaps the teacher.

But let's say Shawn creates the picture in this context: the teacher has reduced the art experience of this child and the group to a "non-art" activity. The intended lesson is to reinforce an association of colors with (stereotypes of) objects in nature.

What color is the sky anyway? Or should we say colors? To get beyond the stereotypical blue, I have asked this question of participants in early childhood (EC) trainings. The responses have included all in a coloring box of twelve, including brown and yellow when there is smog and green in a tornado sky. Even young children have seen many of these colors. Why encourage children to accept a stereotype even if innocuous rather than the whole wonderous reality? In this situation, is it they or us who "can't handle the truth"?

It is a "follow-directions, color-object correspondence, eye-hand coordination" lesson. The teacher shows a model picture with a blue sky, yellow sun, green grass, brown tree trunk, lollipop green foliage, and red apples for the children to copy (sound familiar?). Each child has a "coloring book" outline of the model picture to work on.

So from the beginning, Shawn gets the lesson wrong—even though the kid incorporated the additional colors of purple and orange and used higher-level thinking skills. The teacher feels obligated to conform to the academic objectives of the lesson and finds it difficult to affirm the child's intelligent but fragile insight. A classmate says, "You did it wrong, Shawn." I cannot think of a more effective way to influence a child toward insecurity around thinking about new ideas and expressing them.

So, all are performing the task "correctly" except Shawn, and one other child, Aaron. Aaron feels unable to duplicate the picture to anyone's satisfaction. Aaron crumples up the outline, throws it on the floor, puts his foot on it, and sits head down at the table.

If programs are not developmentally appropriate, they can cause passive-aggressive *mistaken behaviors* in the group. Most children will tend toward the passive/conformist end of the spectrum, likely with latent resentment about the teacher's mistrust of their creative abilities (that at some point will express itself). Some children will tend toward the aggressive/oppositional end, like Aaron. For all the children, the teacher's decision to conform to a preset lesson happens at the expense of emotional/social and cognitive development and causes mistaken behavior—feelings of inadequacy that are internalized, angrily expressed, or both. I call this classroom-caused mistaken behavior, caused by the teacher.

When teachers overtly or unintentionally repress children's expression of ideas, they contribute to their stress and undermine self-esteem. Teachers cannot practice guidance in situations when they themselves have influenced children toward conforming or oppositional mistaken behaviors. They can only practice guidance in programs that are developmentally appropriate and encourage significant learning in every child.

I used art versus non-art for illustration here because art represents the child's foundational efforts at expressing ideas on paper. Art is the young child's celebration of life, lament, journal entry, story, poem. In their books, children see that art tells stories, and as natural storytellers, they want to try this themselves. Do we impose "logical" academic standards on the first written-down expressions of children or allow the dynamic of natural psychological development to come through? The job of the teacher is to take logically constructed curriculum and psychologize it so the child can find meaningful experiences in classroom activities. Artistic and overall expressive development comes with creative opportunity and encouragement. (Question to readers: Was this rant justified?)

## What Readiness Is

When they enter the next level of education, we want children to be confident and competent in their learning endeavors. In the guidance perspective, what children know is not as important as their being willing and capable when they encounter what they *do not* know. In guidance terms, readiness is being confident and competent in the face of new learning experiences. This mental state of readiness derives from secure relationships with significant adults who are responsive to the unique learning endeavors of each child. Readiness, like guidance, has its foundation in secure child-adult relationships.

Again, in the guidance perspective, what children know is not as important as their being willing and capable when they encounter what they *do not* know. In guidance terms, readiness is being confident and competent in the face of new learning experiences.

Developmentally appropriate practice is the pathway to readiness. When using DAP, teachers hold the child to be more important than the curriculum. They see their job as mediating between the psychological child and the logical curriculum in ways that further secure relationships and to empower readiness. Thanks to John Dewey for giving voice to this idea more than eighty years ago (1938) in the teaching process he called *psychologizing the curriculum*.

## Beyond a "Content" Definition

With this overview, the article that forms the basis of chapter 5 starts here, further exploring the interconnection of readiness, guidance, and DAP. (Thanks to NAEYC for permission to reuse the article—which has the same title as this chapter. This iteration includes slight editing.)

It used to be that people thought children were ready for school if they could say (and sound) their ABCs, count, identify colors, and print their names. Yet readiness isn't just knowing the "preacademic" basics. Readiness always has been more complicated than this, and new brain research is spelling out what readiness really is.

We know now that readiness is a *mental set of willingness and confidence* when it comes to learning: readiness is a state of mind. We also know that every learning act has an emotional as well as a cognitive dimension. Significant learning, the kind that stays with a child for its positive meaning, happens when the child feels positively about the learning experience. DAP provides such learning opportunities. Personal, meaningful learning experiences create a willingness and confidence in the child, allowing them to flourish as a continuing learner, which is the state of mind that we call "readiness."

But even before developmentally appropriate programs, building secure relationships with each child is where we start. Children need to know that significant adults are totally on their side. Children who know they are accepted and appreciated have an easier time engaging in learning activities.

Children who feel constantly, or even often, stressed in relation to these basic needs have a much more difficult time. The reason is that the amygdala-driven survival system of the brain is more developed in young children than their thinking and learning systems. Young children sense threat easily. *Adverse experiences* make the stress they feel unmanageable and hard to shake, overwhelming a healthy ability to learn.

Teachers dedicated to building readiness in children have a twofold task: (1) through relationship-based teaching, guide children to manage their stress and feel they are worthy members of the group and (2) nudge children into engaging with, and gaining from, developmentally appropriate learning experiences and therefore building healthy states of mind.

## Six Teaching Practices That Support Learning and Empower Readiness

Below are six teaching practices that support children in the learning act and empower readiness for further learning. (Reference notes at the end of this chapter provide follow-up resources.)

# 1. Use "Acknowledge and Pause"

Acknowledge and pause (AAP) is a simple but profound place to begin. Acknowledge the child with a compliment and then pause, which gives the child a chance to respond. AAP tells the child that the leader cares enough to pay attention. It is a sure relationship starter—and so much more authentic than adults' conventional mental shortcut, "Good job."

Five of the six practices have been introduced in earlier chapters of this book. We authors call such repeat appearances not repetition, but reinforcement of important concepts. :-}). The five practices are particularly useful in building readiness as a state of mind.

AAP is a helpful response when an adult wants to recognize a child's efforts but isn't sure what to say (like pre-representational art). Before the pause, offer a friendly comment about the details you see. A useful starter stem is: "You are really . . ."

- using lots of blue.

- climbing high on that "jungle gym."

- helping to clean up.

- looking like you have tears on your face.

- helping Clarence with that iPad.

Illustration: To thirty-eight-month-old Leon, who is drawing a big corkscrew shape with a brown marker, "You are really drawing all over that big paper!" After a pause, Leon responds, "Yup, this is Cleo [big sister]. She got her car, and she is driving all over the place." To which the adult nods and gives a smile (important practices in themselves) and says, "Cleo's driving on that road. Bet she is driving fast." After another brief pause, Leon says, "Yep, she drives really fast! It was broke but it's runnin' good now."

The interaction empowers the child to practice thinking and communication skills—not to mention creative abilities. These interactions build brains. With this kind of encouragement, the child will keep wanting to draw "story pictures" (pictures that tell stories—like in books). In a year or so, another picture of Cleo and her car will look entirely different. It might even have a letter like C and the child's own printed name.

Teachers use AAP to recognize actions, thoughts, and feelings. (When acknowledging feelings, some use the terms *reflective listening* or *perspective-taking*.) The friendly exchange that AAP kindles often grows into a *contact talk* and generates an instant connection between the two individuals.

## 2. Have Contact Talks with Each Child Every Day

A contact talk is a shared quality moment between an adult and a child. For contact talks to happen, the adult who is approached must decide to listen to and talk with the child. During a contact talk, the adult does not teach, preach, or screech, but listens, encourages, and supports. The purpose is to learn more about this little person and have that child learn more about you as a leader in the community life you share.

Contact talks build healthy relationships between adults and children like nothing else can. The talks support the development of self-esteem, social skills, thinking skills, vocabulary, and communication abilities (all key capacities for school success).

Contact talks can happen at any time (e.g., while reading together, changing diapers, during active play, or when children arrive [important!]). Though appearing to be difficult to fit in, these "greeting" talks are worth the time. They are an investment in the child, and they ease children into the program each day.

Contact talks don't have to be long, but they do need to happen with every child every day. Contact talks tell children they are valued, what they say is worthwhile, and that they belong in the group. Plus, they provide a way for the teacher to get to know those children who are hard to understand and help the children get to know the teacher and feel that they belong in the program. Even if brief, a contact talk is a gift of time to a child. So many readiness abilities come alive from contact talks. Below is a sample interaction.

To illustrate, let us return to the case of Shawn and the many-colored sky—but this time *not from the context of a close-ended lesson but instead a brain-building, open-ended creative experience*. Probably with a different teacher, Shawn then could participate in a contact talk that might go like this:

TEACHER: You are really using every color in that box for your sky, Shawn. (Pauses.)

SHAWN: Yup, I'm using all the colors because the sky isn't just blue, you know.

TEACHER: You know the sky is many colors. *I wonder* how you know that?

SHAWN: 'Cause me and my family saw the sun go down, and it was beeuutiful!

TEACHER: I bet it was. I bet you saw many colors.

SHAWN: Yeah, and I got them all in my picture, and there was even brown and green.

TEACHER: Brown and green in the sky? (Thinking of smog and "tornado" clouds.)

SHAWN: No, brown and green was on the ground, but there wasn't gray.

TEACHER (smiling): There wasn't gray?

SHAWN: No, the sky wasn't gray, like today with them clouds.

(Shawn goes back to coloring. Teacher moves over to Aaron.)

Author's note: So much for the original teacher's objective of color-to-object correspondence—demonstrated here through creative and not teacher-structured activity. Bet *this* teacher also gets Aaron back to coloring.

Note to readers: Contact talks at first seem like a challenge. But if you dedicate yourself to trying them, with practice they become easier and natural. As a teenager once told me, "Nothing to it but to do it."

## 3. Accommodate Early Reasoning Skills

Reasoning ability, what many call "executive function," starts to develop in the brain at about age three years. Reasoning skills, including the capacity to understand others' viewpoints and to stay on task, are a work in progress into adulthood.

Young children do not have the same grasp of reality as adults. They see things from their own charming viewpoints. An example is young Virgil, who explains what makes the wind blow: "De trees push de air." An encouraging response is to smile, nod, and say, "I never thought of it that way, Virgil. I wonder how that happens." Virgil patiently explains, "De leaves is fans of course!" Just enjoy and encourage the child's dynamic thinking, making as your priority the human connection, not "fact checking" young brains. Don't worry, the child will think differently about the wind in a few years. By the way, what does make the wind blow anyway?

Brain development is at its peak, but also is most vulnerable, during early childhood. Think of behaviors often considered to be "misbehaviors," as *mistaken behaviors*. It is an error for adults to conclude that children misbehave because they "know better" and have chosen to do wrong. Young children have conflicts—disagreements with others—because their incomplete brain development and limited experience mean they *don't* know how to behave better.

An earlier example is Aaron and his crumpled picture. We work on how to express strong emotions in nonhurting ways—including to ourselves—for our entire lives. Young children are just beginning to learn this complicated skill. They are going to make mistakes, sometimes spectacular ones. When an adult holds children's mistakes against them, their progress toward readiness becomes a challenge. Accepting them as months-old beings who are learning a lot but have a lot to learn helps them get past conflicts and back to learning.

## 4. Even During Conflicts, Teach in Firm but Friendly Ways

One of the problems with conventional discipline is that it too easily slides into punishment. In preschool, the most common punishment is embarrassment—calling out kids' names, correcting children in front of others, using time-outs. Research shows that punishment harms healthy brain development. Stress reactions from punishment override children's developing ability to listen to others' viewpoints and use reason to solve problems—the very brain functions we want children to learn.

No one is to be harmed in the EC community. When children make mistakes and cause conflicts, there are consequences, *but the consequences are for the adult as well as the child*. The consequence for the adult is to teach the child to express strong emotions in ways that aren't harmful. The consequence for the child is to understand the adult's firm and friendly expectation that he or she can learn another way.

To teach during conflicts, the first step is to calm everyone down, including yourself. Time away from the situation may be important for calming young children down. *This is not a time-out for something a child has done* but a cooling-down time so all can get calm, talk about what happened, and learn a better way for next time.

Your ability to calm children depends on the relationships you have built with them *outside of conflict situations*. If kids know we care about them, even imperfect efforts at guidance work wonders. Friendly humor is a key tool in all kinds of situations. With strong conflicts, four important guidance practices are group meetings, guidance talks, conflict mediation, and comprehensive guidance. Each method begins with de-escalation—calming everyone down. Leaders who guide children toward perspective-taking and problem-solving are teaching a most fundamental readiness skill. Consider a child in a class of thirty kindergartners with one teacher.

## 5. Use Developmentally Appropriate Practice with Every Child

Two points are most important here:

1.  Young children learn through their bodies, through movement of their large and small muscle groups. Young children need EC programs that are less like traditional classrooms and more like summer camp. They need big-body activity. Research is beginning to show that preschoolers who have active lives—are up and moving and doing less seat work—are able to stay on-task

longer when they are in elementary school. Plus, they have a head start on developing active lifestyles and keeping weight in check. To be inclusive of children who seem restless, bored, or "flighty," *make the program more active*. (Refer to Guidance Matters Column #14.)

2. Young children cannot easily replicate (copy) teacher-made models (e.g., Thanksgiving turkeys) and commercial models (e.g., a picture on a construction box of the *Millennium Falcon*). You wouldn't expect pre-K children to write cursively, so don't push kids into projects they are not ready for by using models with academic preset outcomes. We want meaningful learning from activities, not teacher-caused failure (children's efforts compared to the model).

Instead, use spoken motivation to nudge children into art, and storage boxes without photos of projects for building. At a class meeting, prompt, "Today in the art center, you can make pictures of what you like to do outside in the snow." Then be charmed by the results: Charlie's green and brown (very thick) "Christmas tree woods." Ida's three snowmobiles on three hills, with two folks on each "sled," evergreen trees in the valleys, and written on the bottom of her story picture, "M n m fm wt snbg." ("Me and my family went snowmobiling.") For those readers in warmer climates, think of your own local outdoor activities.

Over time children's art becomes more sophisticated expression. Christmas tree scribbles become distinct forms become early pictorial story pictures like Ida's. Personal script becomes random letters, becomes significant letters, becomes words that are inventively spelled—the pathway to written expression. And, with adult encouragement, children's confidence in their ability to express ideas on paper is sustained.

## 6. Build Partnerships with Families

Families are the prime movers, of course, when it comes to a child's readiness. Family members spending quality time talking with their children, reading to them, appreciating their creative doings—these efforts make all the difference. Many families simply do not know that these simple activities, based on secure relationships with their children, do so much to build readiness. What makes an EC teacher's job both important and difficult is leading parents to both gain and use this knowledge.

I use a four-level gauge to assess how well EC leaders are succeeding in gaining family engagement with the program. The higher the engagement level, the more the whole family, and especially young children, are likely to benefit. The four levels of parent engagement, to be discussed more in chapter 6, are

1. willingness to receive program information;

2. engaging in the education and development of the child;

3. participating in program activities that touch more than the family's own child; and

4. parent self-involvement in personal and professional development as a result of program participation.

The main step that makes a difference in families' ability to help their children gain readiness is the move from level 1 to level 2. To support families in progressing to level 2, EC leaders build partnerships with them, working relationships built on trust.

Family life has never been simple. Today family life is more complicated than ever. The mix of family structures in an EC community is often complex, including surrogate parents (e.g., grandparents), single parents, blended families, and families with their own particular linguistic, racial, religious, cultural, socioeconomic, gender-related, and occupation backgrounds.

Partnerships start with, and rely on, teachers' reaching out in friendly ways to family members. ("Be friendly first!") Especially when families first start the program, EC leaders work to build connections through greeting meetings, conferences (held in comfortable places for families), happy grams (written compliments sent home with the child), phone calls and messages, and whatever techy communication practices (if any) the family is used to—used regularly for positive messages home and to set up conferences. Again, the teacher takes these steps to help parents move from a level of accepting information but taking minimal initiative to recognizing they are on the same team as the teacher and working together on behalf of the child.

In this effort, teachers work hard not to give up on any family. They know they are making progress when family members open up in talking about their children. Leaders know parents are moving to the second level when they begin to ask questions about things they can do with their children and report on things they have done. When families reach level 2, teachers have earned a big beverage of their choice!

Whatever the family situation, family members are the first and foremost teachers of their children. Early childhood professionals only help. In building readiness in children, teachers accomplish with families what they cannot accomplish alone. The family-teacher connection in building readiness is vital, and for this reason the teacher-family partnership is the focus of the next chapter.

# Wrap-Up

Readiness is a state of mind. It is a child's capability and confidence in the face of new learning opportunities. Guidance, DAP, and readiness are interconnected. When adults use guidance, and young children have a plethora of DA learning experiences, children will be ready to succeed at the next level. Six practices consistently used by adults build readiness skills:

1. relying on the practice of "acknowledge and pause";

2. having contact talks with each child every day;

3. remembering that children's reasoning skills are just beginning to develop;

4. teaching in firm and friendly ways during conflicts;

5. using DAP with every child; and

6. building partnerships with families.

The central readiness question is not what children know, but what their confidence and competence levels are when encountering what they have yet to learn. Children who are ready for the next level have fundamentally achieved democratic life skills 1 and 2 and are making solid progress with DLS 3, 4, and 5.

**Take-away question:** How do you see DAP, guidance, and readiness connecting in your setting?

## Reference Notes

The most recent expression of these ideas is in my 2017 Redleaf Press book, *Guidance for Every Child: Teaching Young Children to Manage Conflict*. For more reading about each of the six principles, check out the following Guidance Matters columns from NAEYC'S *Young Children* magazine. The columns, training handouts, and book information can be downloaded from www.dangartrell.net.

1. Use the practice of "acknowledge and pause."

   Column #10, "'You Really Worked Hard on Your Picture': Guiding with Encouragement"

2. Have contact talks with each child every day.

    Column #6, "Building Relationships through Talk"

3. Remember that children's reasoning skills are just beginning to develop.

    Column #3, "Boys and Men Teachers"

    Column #11, "He Did It on Purpose!"

    Column #27, "Guidance with Girls"

4. Even during conflicts, teach in firm and friendly ways.

    Column #3, "A Student Teacher Uses Conflict Mediation"

    Column #5, "A Spoonful of Laughter"

    Column #13, "Comprehensive Guidance"

    Column #18, "Aggression, the Prequel"

5. Use DAP with every child.

    Column #14, "Promote Physical Activity. It's Proactive Guidance"

    Column #19, "From Rules to Guidelines: Moving to the Positive"

6. Build partnerships with parents.

    Column #13, "Comprehensive Guidance"

    Column #18, "Aggression, the Prequel"

    Column #20, "'Goodest' Guidance: Teachers and Families Together"

Dewey, John. 1938. *Experience and Education*. Indianapolis, IN: Kappa Delta Pi.

Rogers, Carl. 1969. *Freedom to Learn*. London: Pearson.

# CHAPTER 6

# Guidance Leadership with Parents

SO, THIS CHAPTER HAS LOTS OF FACTS, figures, and direct quotes. I know, I know. But this information will have meaning for you, and it sets up the rest of the discussion like nothing else can.

Before the stats though, as this is the chapter on families, I'd like to start with the definition of the term *parent* used in the book. It is used inclusively, referring to one or more family members who are the primary caregivers to children. Most clearly it includes birth parents, single parents, stepparents, and adoptive parents. But the term also encompasses surrogate parents—family members other than birth parents who have assumed parental responsibility for children. We are also including under this label foster parents for their necessary, but difficult, role in a substitute home that is not natural to the child.

When surrogate parents raise children, it is usually because a defining tragedy has occurred in the family. Persons not naturally in the role have stepped forward in a major way. Surrogate parents face multiple challenges because they are not naturally cast in this role. Often they are elderly and/or with limited income. In addition to the challenge of radically changed family dynamics, surrogate parents frequently experience withheld recognition and support from outside of the family because they are not the "real" parents. When an early childhood leader meets surrogate parents, she or he should be especially inclusive toward them; they are trying as hard as they can in a difficult job they volunteered for but did not expect. The circumstances sometimes are sad.

> Some ideas in this chapter were given prior expression in *Guidance for Every Child: Teaching Young Children to Manage Conflict* (2017) and *A Guidance Approach for an Encouraging Classroom* (2013).

A single parent of two young children dies in an accident. Her retired mother, an immigrant without a pension and with a long-past substance dependency, begins to raise the children. She runs into roadblocks in terms of adoption proceedings, social services, her dubious friends, and the still-in-shock children.

It is worth remembering that single parents, biological or surrogate, are working "twice as hard." (For the first ten years of my life, my mother was a single parent, so I know firsthand.) You might be acquainted with single parents who are keeping their families amazingly intact (thanks, Mom), and two-parent families, even if well off, that are cracked or even broken—even if the factures do not readily show. Balancing the "they're everywhere" demands of modern life is hard enough for two parents; the demands are multiplied when there is only one.

Young teacher Amy enjoyed having Kenny in her group. Amy was disappointed, though, when mother Sheryl did not make the program's "greeting meetings" (held at two different times). Sheryl also did not reply to Amy's phone calls, messages, and texts about the start-up parent-teacher conference. Amy mentioned her frustration to a trusted veteran teacher, who commented, "Oh, didn't you know? Sheryl works as a waitress afternoons and nights at the bar Louie's. The kids go to their grandma's after school. Mom often crashes there too."

Knowing this, Amy called Sheryl at the bar, said how much she enjoyed Kenny, and asked if maybe they could have a get-acquainted conference where Sheryl worked. Sheryl was dubious, but Amy gently nudged, "Maybe on your break? Could you ask your boss? I'll hold." Sheryl reluctantly asked. The boss said sure, she could meet the teacher on her break. Amy and Sheryl met in an empty booth.

The two hit it off and met a few other times at the bar during the fall. One concrete result was that Sheryl saw the importance of her mother reading to the children before bed, which Grandma enjoyed doing. Amy drank more diet root beers at the bar than usual but was pleased with the meetings.

After Thanksgiving, Sheryl accepted a repeated invitation from Amy. Sheryl came into the classroom before her shift and, with Kenny on her lap, read to a group of children. Sheryl had a good time, and the visits became a regular event. Amy and Sheryl built a secure relationship that lasted all year. Kenny blossomed.

Almost all families care about their children. If they do not respond as EC providers would like, it is usually because they are busy to the point of overload trying to keep a roof overhead, food on the table, reliable transportation, medical bills covered, child care fees paid, and a nondelinquent cell phone account. (Among the basic needs of adults these days.)

## Families of the Twenty-First Century: Diversity, the New "Typical"

EC leaders have a handle on the types of families they serve. The families range from mostly homogenous, in many rural areas and communities predominantly of one cultural group, to way-diverse in many cities and towns. Multiracial families tend to, but not always, follow these geographical markers as well. The website of the American Academy of Pediatrics (healthychildren.org) provides "A Family Portrait" of different family types nationally.

**Nuclear Families**: Approximately half of all families with youngsters under age eighteen are composed of two biological parents and their children.

**Single-Parent Families:** Single-parent families make up 27 percent of households with children under age eighteen.

**Blended Families:** About 20 percent of children in two-parent households live in blended families.

**Same-Sex Parent Families:** Some two million children have parents who are lesbian, gay, bisexual, transgender, or queer (LGBTQ).

**Never-Married Families:** About 1.5 million unmarried couples have at least one child under age fifteen.

**Cross-Generational Families:** Approximately 670,000 families with children under age eighteen have a family member aged sixty-five or older living with them. Roughly 2.5 million children under age eighteen live with one or both parents in their grandparents' home.

**Grandparents as Parents:** Approximately 1.3 million children under age eighteen live with their grandparents.

**Adoptive/Foster Families:** Approximately 120,000 children are adopted each year. For every 1,000 children, 6.3 live in out-of-home foster care.

In other words, more than half of American families that used to be considered "not typical" are "typical." These newly typical families might be a sizable number in any particular EC community.

Within the EC community, each unique family structure poses its own potential challenges for staff and other parents. How could established traditional families pose challenges? Think about possible resentments by adult early childhood education (ECE) community members toward affluent parents who regularly try to "influence" the program. The challenge is to be friendly with all families and uniformly supportive of all children—without favoritism for social as well as psychological reasons. Leaders do well to recognize the types of family structures represented in the program as they become acquainted and work with their individual families.

## Three Hundred Languages

Another diversity factor in modern families is the increase in different languages spoken in the home. The Census Bureau released data from the 2013 American Community Survey, including languages spoken for those five years of age and older. The data show that the number of people who speak a language other than English at home reached an all-time high of 61.8 million, up 2.2 million since 2010. Among the findings: Languages with more than one million speakers in 2013 were Spanish (38.4 million), Mandarin (3 million), Tagalog (1.6 million), Vietnamese (1.4 million), French (1.3 million), and Korean and Arabic (1.1 million each). Tagalog is the national language of the Philippines. Of school-aged children nationally, more than one in five speak a foreign language at home (44 percent in California and roughly one in three students in Texas, Nevada, and New York). But more surprisingly, it is now one in seven students in Georgia, North Carolina, Virginia, Nebraska, and Delaware and one out of eight students in Kansas, Utah, Minnesota, and Idaho. Many of those who speak a foreign language at home are not immigrants. Of the nearly 62 million foreign-language speakers, 44 percent (27.2 million) were born in the United States. States with the largest share of foreign-language speakers in 2013 included California, 45 percent; New Mexico, 36 percent; Texas, 35 percent; New Jersey, 30 percent; Nevada, 30 percent; New York, 30 percent; Florida, 27 percent; Arizona, 27 percent; Hawaii, 25 percent; Illinois, 23 percent; Massachusetts, 22 percent; Connecticut, 22 percent; and Rhode Island, 21 percent.

Two major groups using home languages other than English should be included in the discussion. The first group is the deaf population, many of whom use American Sign Language (ASL). Even with my editors' assistance, it has been difficult to determine the numbers of persons who are deaf and the numbers of those folks who use ASL. In 2010 the US Census continued the practice of omitting questions about American Sign and other deaf/hearing-impaired communication systems in the area of languages spoken. Beyond the US census, there have been insufficient resources for other public and private organizations to conduct the exhaustive research necessary to determine these numbers. Three complicating factors are these: (1) Many people face hearing loss and deafness only later in life. (2) Writers have conflated users of American Sign with the larger deaf population who may use other systems or none at all. (3) Erroneous characterizations about numbers have been used and have taken on a life of their own, such as "American Sign is the third most spoken language in the U.S." No known studies back this claim—which until very recently I believed was true. (See Mitchell in "Reference Notes" on page 91. The research is from 2006, but the problems largely remain.)

Whatever the number, many EC communities have families with children who show hearing disabilities and might well be using American Sign at home. The benefits for this population of teaching ASL as a second language are similar to those of children who speak any heritage language that is not English. But there are other demonstrated benefits of teaching American Sign in early childhood programs. Signing is an easy mode of communication to learn for toddlers with emerging language, non-English-speaking preschoolers, and young children in general for whom speaking oral English is proving difficult. Sign can serve as a "bridging language" in early childhood that other languages perhaps cannot. This benefit of teaching and learning sign in early childhood should not be underestimated.

The second group is American Indian families who speak the original languages of North America. In a 2020 work on indigenous languages, Ojibwe scholar Anton Treuer estimates that of 500 native languages "before contact," only about 150 remain. (See reference notes.) While, sadly, many of these languages are still dying out, the Ojibwe and Lakota in the upper Midwest, the Seminole in the Southeast, the Navaho in the Southwest, and the Iroquois tribes in the Northeast, among other American Indian nations, are taking steps to teach young children their Native tongues. Immersion schools in Native languages (as well as in many other languages) are on the increase. Including the languages of the First Peoples, probably more than three hundred languages other than English are spoken in U.S. homes today.

For more information, check out the website of the ASL and English Bilingual Consortium for Early Childhood Education at bilingualece.org.

The Concordia College Language Villages near Bemidji, Minnesota, offer immersion camp experiences for children and teens in fifteen languages. Each language has its own camp, and the program bills itself as "North America's premier language and cultural program" for young people. Our own family has three members who attended the Language Villages. After going for five years, one of them completed secondary school, a baccalaureate, and a master's program in Germany (daughter Kateri spoke no German before going to language camp). (For the author, the Language Villages program will become "extra premier" when it establishes language camps in Ojibwe and Lakota—Minnesota's two main indigenous communities.)

## Becoming Bilingual

While English is the primary language of the United States, I have always considered those who speak another language as having a special gift. To squelch a myth, few, if any, young children who speak other languages at home have trouble learning "American" (as our eldest granddaughter, at age seven, once informed a class of mine. Julia grew up largely in Germany. She had been told more than once there, "You don't speak English, you speak 'American'").

Over the last thirty years, a multitude of studies have documented the benefits of becoming multilingual, especially early in life. The American Council on the Teaching of Foreign Languages provides a useful summary of many studies. Two inquiry questions frame the findings of the summary:

1. How does language learning support academic achievement?

2. How does language learning provide cognitive benefits to students?

*Question 1 Findings: How does language learning support academic achievement?*

- Language learning correlates with higher academic achievement on standardized test measures.

- Language learning is beneficial in the development of students' reading abilities.

- There is evidence that language learners transfer skills from one language to another.

- There is a correlation between second language learning and increased linguistic awareness.

- There is a correlation between language learning and students' ability to hypothesize in science.

- Heritage learners who use their language skills to interpret and translate for family members experience higher academic performance and greater self-efficacy.

*Question 2 Findings: How does language learning provide cognitive benefits to students?*

- There is evidence that early language learning improves cognitive abilities.

- There is a correlation between bilingualism and attentional control on cognitive tasks (healthy operation of executive function).

- There is a correlation between bilingualism and metalinguistic skills.

- There is a correlation between bilingualism and memory skills.

- There is a correlation between bilingualism and problem-solving ability.

- There is a correlation between bilingualism and improved verbal and spatial abilities.

- There is a correlation between bilingualism and the offset [delay] of age-related cognitive losses like dementia and Alzheimer's. (Yep, you read that right!)

In the online version of the council's summary, each statement is hot-linked to supporting references (www.actfl.org/advocacy/what-the-research-shows).

In addition, the council provides hot-linked studies that point to the conclusion that language learners develop positive cultural awareness toward the second language and the speakers of that language. This conclusion follows well from a study published in the *New York Times* (2016) titled "The Superior Social Skills of Bilinguals." In relation to the enhanced social skills shown by bilingual children in a diverse group of four- to six-year-olds, Kinzler explains:

> Children in multilingual environments have social experiences that provide routine practice in considering the perspectives of others: They have to think about who speaks which language to whom, who understands which content, and the times and places in which different languages are spoken.

Before age five, young children are able to empower the same mental dynamic that develops one language to other languages as well. Bialystok (2015) points out that while a young child's vocabularies in both languages might be delayed a bit, "their understanding of linguistic structure, called metalinguistic awareness, is at least as good and often better than that of comparable monolinguals." In addition, the vocabulary delay reverses in favor of dual language learners in a year or two.

One other lightbulb factor makes learning multiple languages in EC the desirable time. Unlike older people, if taught in supportive ways, preschoolers do not worry if they make mistakes in their language learning. This anxiety is a major deterrent to older folks learning a second language, which maybe some of us have experienced. Young children don't worry about mistakes. They just go ahead and learn the "next" language.

As a guy who speaks only "American" and remembers just a few Ojibwe words (like *waabooz*—"rabbit") from my Head Start teaching days, my position about teaching multiple languages in EC should now be clear. (It is why we took this "scenic route" in a chapter on working with parents.) If one or more learning community members speaks a language other than spoken English at home, make this *heritage language* part of your education program. Build on the community resources you can find—especially parents—and use practices such as those mentioned on the helpful 2019 NAEYC website "Welcoming and Supporting Dual Language Learners." Make the heritage language of some children an opportunity for all the learning community to become dual language learners.

The NAEYC webpage is https://naeyc.org/resources/topics/dual-language-learners. The webpage shares content with the May issue of NAEYC's *Young Children*. This issue "includes a cluster of articles on cultivating bilingualism and the benefits of multilingual classrooms."

The adults in your community will be the only ones who worry about mistakes in the language learning. And think about how the families speaking that other language in the home will feel: fully included. This endeavor takes a lot of effort, I know. But the benefits are many:

- Young children are using (and so growing) their brains more fully, to their lifelong benefit.

- Parents who speak the other languages at home feel more fully engaged in the EC community.

- Parents in general are amazed that their children are picking up another language "so easily" and may learn a bit of it themselves. Members of the outside community are impressed that your program is multilingual.

Teaching a second language is a special way to bring together children and adults in the EC community. For many reasons, the practice benefits the whole community, especially families from heritage language homes.

## Poverty, the Confounding Factor

Poverty confounds modern family life. Most countries trying to remediate this problem do not have the diversity, history, and politics of the United States. The resulting complex of dynamics is why other countries do better than the United States at responding to the problem of wage disparity. To give a proper overview of this US issue, let's turn to the ultimate source for many, the Children's Defense Fund annual report, "The State of America's Children 2020."

> The selected passages from the 2020 report tell the story far better than I could and in half as many words. Readers can access the tables referred to and the full report at www.childrensdefense .org/the-state-of-americas-children-2020.

Children remain the poorest age group in America. Nearly 1 in 6 lived in poverty in 2018—nearly 11.9 million children (see Table 2). Children are considered poor if they live in a family with an annual income below the Federal Poverty Line of $25,701 for a family of four, which amounts to less than $2,142 a month, $494 a week or $70 a day (see Table 3). Child poverty is related to both age and race/ethnicity. The youngest children are the poorest and nearly 73 percent of poor children in America are children of color. Nearly 1 in 3 Black (30.1 percent) and American Indian/Alaska Native children (29.1 percent) and nearly 1 in 4 Hispanic children (23.7 percent) were poor compared with 1 in 11 white children (8.9 percent) (see Tables 5–6).

Every year children spend in poverty is dangerous and expensive. The toxic stress of early poverty stunts children's development, creating opportunity gaps that can last a lifetime and harm the nation's economy.

Poor children are more likely to have poor academic achievement, drop out of high school and later become unemployed, experience economic hardship and be involved in the criminal justice system. Children who experience poverty are also more likely to be poor at age 30 than children who never experience poverty.

Lost productivity, worsened health and increased crime stemming from child poverty cost the nation about $700 billion dollars a year, or about 3.5 percent of GDP.

The trials of poverty weigh heavily on all members of low-income families. In working with all families, especially those facing poverty, three mantras of guidance leadership apply: "Listen before you speak." "Be friendly first." "Be unrelentingly positive." (Thanks to Marian Marion for the last one.)

# Engaging with Families

We look at two topics in particular in this section: parent-teacher conferences and a four-level model for parent engagement.

## Parent-Teacher Conferences

Except for home visits, conferences provide the most direct link between teacher and parent. Much has been written about parent-teacher conferences. Gonzalez-Mena (2014) emphasizes that EC professionals need to see themselves as learners as well as teachers, especially when cultural differences, including a home language other than English, are involved. Gestwicki (2015) suggests that successful conferences consist of three phases: preparing, conducting, and evaluating.

> The section on conferences is adapted from my 2017 book. Thanks to Redleaf Press for letting me share this material in slightly updated form.

*Preparing for the Conference*

When preparing, the teacher needs to make sure parents know the reasons for the conference. A program guidebook that is gone over at a greeting meeting with groups and individual families can include a statement about conferences. If possible, the guidebook should be in the home languages of the program's children and families. Time options for conferences are important, including both evening and daytime slots if possible. Leaders should plan adequate time for the discussion so parents do not feel hurried—conferences might be spread out over a few weeks.

Teachers should determine if parents want information shared in hardcopy or via an electronic device.

Providing a comfortable setting for parent conferences is important. An informal, private setting, in which parents and teacher can sit side by side at a table, is preferable to conversing across a desk. At one parent's suggestion, a teacher held conferences in a small parents' corner already established in the room. The corner included bulletin board dividers, two easy chairs, and a coat rack. The parents loved the change.

A mother named Arnetta shared with the teacher that her husband, Voshon, literally had a gag reflex when he entered the doors of the school—which he had attended—due to his own distressing experiences as a student there. The teacher suggested that they have the initial conference in a neighborhood fast-food restaurant. Arnetta got Voshon to attend, and the teacher emphasized her positive perceptions of how their son, Tori, was doing. Dad later decided he could make the next conference in the classroom—the teacher had communicated clearly and consistently to him that their son was an accepted and respected member of the class.

For the conference, the teacher should have a folder or electronic portfolio for each child with samples of the child's work over a period of time, including photographs and/or videos of the child's activities and projects. If using an electronic device, a laptop or large-screen tablet is important. (A larger screen displays better than a smart phone.) Pictorial samples are particularly useful when holding conferences with parents who speak limited English. A form or device to record notes from the conference rounds out this stage (Gestwicki 2015).

*Conducting the Conference*

For the conduct of the conference, the teacher sets the tone with positive statements about the child, such as, "I really enjoy having Maya in class. She seems to love school and has such a sense of humor." The teacher asks the parents to share what they would like to see the conference accomplish. The teacher goes over the materials she has prepared and invites the parents to discuss them. When the leader talks about the child, she or he uses the technique discussed in chapter 2 called the *compliment sandwich*—giving *at least* two positive statements about the child's effort and progress that frame one suggestion for further growth.

The teacher also encourages family members to share information about their child's home life. She or he acknowledges the parents' comments and uses *reflective listening*, a variation of acknowledge and pause, which means repeating back the thoughts and feelings the other person is expressing and then giving time for a reply. Reflective listening helps ensure that the parents' messages have been received as intended. As the conference wraps up, the teacher summarizes decisions made and follow-up plans, checking to make sure family members agree. The teacher ends the conference on a positive note (Gestwicki 2015). (Just maybe not with balloons and bouquets—in most situations.)

An important trend in parent-teacher conferences is to include the learner along with the parents. Leaders' first reactions to this idea might be guarded; they (and the parents) have to approach both the material and the communication process differently with the learner present. After teachers get used to this format, they commonly say that under most circumstances, they wouldn't have conferences any other way. Often a young child will sit in on part of the conference, then be free to play in the room if the discussion gets too involved.

### Evaluating the Conference

Following the conference, the teacher evaluates the session by reviewing notes and completing a brief summary—in hardcopy or electronically. She or he files a copy and sends a copy to the parents—in their home language when possible, and at the level of technology the family is comfortable with. The teacher reflects in personal terms about the success of the conference, carries through on agreed-upon follow-up actions, and initiates plans for conferences to come.

It can be tempting to regard the meeting and its evaluation as the conclusion of the effort to build productive relations with families, but collaborative teacher-parent relations are an ongoing effort. When EC professionals carry through with follow-ups and further conferences, they show they understand the importance of the family in the life of the child and in the EC community.

## A Model for Parent Engagement

A four-level model for encouraging and tracking parent engagement has been featured in my writing for years and was introduced in chapter 5. I like the model because it provides a conscious and intentional plan for reaching out and including families in the EC community. It also provides an informal assessment tool for how much engagement a family might be showing. Written about more fully in *Guidance for Every Child* (2017), the model explicates four levels of parent engagement:

Level 1: Accepting Program Information

Level 2: Active Educational Engagement with One's Child

Level 3: Active Program Participation

Level 4: Personal-Professional Development

Early childhood programs should work for all parents to reach level 2 within the first year. All programs can also encourage parents to reach level 3. Parents tend to reach level 4 in programs with intentional and planned active parent-involvement components. If some readers began as volunteers in EC settings and now are EC professionals, you have reached the top of the ladder, level 4. Congratulations! How is the view? Bet you have already thanked those host teachers.

Let's use a previous anecdote with Teacher Amy and single parent and waitress Sheryl to illustrate teacher responses and resulting parent behaviors that indicate progress in reaching the levels. I'll wait if you want to go back and read it again (see page 76 :-}).

## Level 1: Accepting Program Information

Sheryl moved to level 1 only after Amy succeeded in contacting her and Sheryl consented to having a conference with Amy in the booth of the bar. Those mantras about listening before speaking, being friendly first, and being unrelentingly positive really fit how Amy worked with Sheryl to assist the parent to gain level 1.

Level 1 is not automatic for parents living in difficult circumstances, of cultural backgrounds different than the teacher's, or with parents like Voshon who had painful experiences in school. Teachers use a variety of proactive practices to convey that the presence of the child in the program is a good thing and that the teacher is making sure that both the child and parent belong. As parents recognize this, it becomes easier for them to learn what the program is about and how they can help their child in the program—making progress toward level 2. On the other hand, some parents will welcome leaders' efforts to build relations and move to level 2 right away.

*Level 2: Active Educational Engagement with One's Child*

With Amy's positive communication about Kenny, Sheryl moved to level 2 when she took an interest in Amy's reports, and the two continued to have meetings in the bar. The key step for all parents is to progress to level 2, as then, and not before, they become willing to team with the teacher in educational engagement with their child.

When parents have reached level 2, they begin to show an interest in their child's activities and become more involved in what they can do at home. Reading to their child nightly is always high on the list, and EC professionals should purposely facilitate this activity. Amy persuaded Sheryl to have her mom start this practice before the kids went to bed at Grandma's. Indirectly, this placed Grandma also at level 2.

If at all possible, the leader should postpone discussions about problems the child might be having until a connection has been made with the parent. The life experience of some parents tells them that any contact by a teacher means criticism of their child.

When leaders decide that a discussion about a problem needs to happen, they set up a face-to-face conference. They don't rely on less-direct communications such as notes, text messages, or phone calls. Teachers use the three-part plan for parent conferences listed under the previous heading, including multiple-layer compliment sandwiches, reflective listening, and working for a cooperative course of action. Early childhood leaders always frame the specific issue that needs to be addressed in the broader context of the child's strengths and positive efforts. This approach improves chances that she or he and the parent are on the same team. Teachers offer suggestions, and get feedback on, ideas for how they can work together. They try hard to accept ideas that parents suggest.

If the leader thinks there is a danger of a personality conflict with one or more family member, she or he might ask that another staff member be present. So as not to appear to gang up on the family, the person's role should be spelled out: just to listen and, as a balanced third party, help the conference along. Administrators or veteran staff members who know the family are naturals to sit in.

With good reason, leaders become wary when they feel they have to recommend testing, outside consultation, or medical examination for a child. The shortcut response regarding this matter is that parents are more receptive to these suggestions when they have come to trust the EC professional—when they have reached engagement level 2.

*Level 3: Active Program Participation*

When Sheryl took Amy's suggestion and came into the room to read to the children on a regular basis, Sheryl had reached level 3. A common expectation regarding level 3 is that parents volunteer in the classroom. Due to work schedules, transportation difficulties, and other factors, some parents can't. But there are other actions parents can take who are at level 3. One is sitting on advisory and planning committees that fit the parent's schedule. Another is helping to round up materials for special projects or volunteering to participate in one-time events.

At least one early group meeting where parents can get to know each other is important for extending the EC community beyond the children in the room. One leader began a greeting meeting by having parents pair off to get to know each other. People introduced themselves in the full group, but the other in the pair then shared something interesting to them about the first person. As a result of one such meeting, a teacher discovered a parent who loved the outdoors. The parent set up outdoor activities like walks in the woods and extended the grateful teacher's resources by recruiting other parents to go with the group.

Teachers often discover that recruiting parents for special events is a better "starter" than expecting modern-day parents to spend regular hours in the classroom. Family members (not necessarily parents) who have interests like carpentry, cooking, sharing a home language, or playing the tuba might volunteer to share their expertise on a one-time basis. And once they get a foot in the door or out in the woods, they are engaging at level 3.

*Level 4: Personal-Professional Development*

In the anecdote, Sheryl continued to come in and read to the group of children. Amy was not aware of other changes in Sheryl in regard to aspects of the parent's personal/professional life. Amy concluded that Sheryl hopefully had made a start on, but had not reached, level 4.

When parents who reach level 4 stay in the EC field, they are a gift. They know what lies ahead of them so much more than young postsecondary graduates (who nonetheless bring wonderful energy and new ideas to the programs they join). If level 4 parents study in ECE preparation programs or train to become child development associates, they bring experiences and understandings with them that will benefit all in the childhood community.

But parents at level 4 can make significant personal/professional gains in other fields as well. Parents who sit on committees that give program input might use and develop skills in technology, accounting, record keeping, or organizing, all of which potentially lead to postsecondary programs and jobs in various fields. For me, a parent who starts by volunteering and ends up getting a GED, becomes proactive in an elementary setting when their child begins school, or leaves with their child from an abusive setting also has gained level 4.

Early childhood leaders who support parents enough for them to gain level 4 often hear, "I am not just telling my kids what they should do anymore; I am showing them. They see that mother or father is doing it, and they think 'I can do it too.'"

Parents who reach level 4 have progressed through the previous three levels thanks to their host EC leaders. Leaders should celebrate when all parents in the community have progressed to level 2, when some parents reach level 3, and, when possible, when one or a few parents have attained level 4. When leaders dedicate themselves to working with parents as well as children, we all benefit.

## Wrap-Up

Chapter 6 used lots of facts, figures, and quotes to emphasize that modern family life is complicated. Whatever the diverse characteristics of the family, leaders need to get to know their families well in order to work with them effectively. Conferences are vital in building partnerships with parents, and successful conferences have three intentional phases: planning, implementation, and follow-up. Using a system of four levels of parent engagement helps carry out and assess successful parent involvement in the program. Parents who reach levels 2, 3, or 4 benefit the child, the family, the program, and the community at large.

Until now, I have not defined an encouraging EC community, though you have figured it out. The definition seems a fitting way to end the chapter.

An encouraging EC community is a physical and social place where young children, family members, and the professionals who serve them all have acceptance as worthy members of the group. It is a friendly setting for living and learning that includes all. Encouraging EC communities begin within the minds of its leaders.

**Take-away question:** How might you use three key ideas from this chapter to further teacher-parent partnerships in your program?

# Reference Notes

American Academy of Pediatrics. 2015. "'A Family Portrait' of Different Family Types Nationally." www.healthychildren.org.

Bialystok, E. "Bilingualism and the Development of Executive Function: The Role of Attention." *Child Development Perspectives*. 9:117–21. https://doi.org/10.1111/cdep.12116.

Children's Defense Fund. 2020. "The State of American Children." www.childrensdefense .org.

Gartrell, Dan. 2017. *Guidance for Every Child: Teaching Young Children to Manage Conflict.* St. Paul, MN: Redleaf Press.

Gestwicki, C. 2015. *Home, School, and Community Relations.* Belmont, CA: Wadsworth /Cengage Learning.

Gonzalez-Mena, J. 2014. *50 Strategies for Communicating and Working with Diverse Families.* 3rd edition. Boston: Pearson.

Kinzler, K. 2016. "The Superior Social Skills of Bilinguals." *New York Times*, March 11, 2016. www.nytimes.com/2016/03/13/opinion/sunday/the-superior-social-skills-of-bilinguals .html.

Lang, S. 2009. "Learning a Second Language Is Good Childhood Mind Medicine, Studies Find." *Cornell Chronicle*, May 12, 2009. www. news.cornell.edu/stories/2009/05 /learning-second-language-good-mind-medicine.

Mitchell, R.E, Young T.A., Bachelda, B., Karchmer, M.A. 2006. "How Many People Use ASL in the United States? Why Estimates Need Updating." *Sign Language Studies* 6, no. 3 (Spring 2006): 306–35. Gallaudet University Press. www.jstor.org/stable /10.2307/26190621.

NAEYC. 2019. "Welcoming and Supporting Dual Language Learners." May 2019. https:// naeyc.org/resources/topics/dual-language-learners. The May 2019 issue of *Young Children* includes a cluster of articles on cultivating bilingualism and the benefits of multilingual classrooms.

Treuer, A. 2020. *The Language Warrior's Manifesto.* St. Paul, MN: Minnesota Historical Society Press.

# CHAPTER 7

# Guidance Leadership with Staff and Outside Professionals

Let's begin this chapter by singing a round of "Kumbaya"! No? Okay. I always listen to my readers most of the time. Staff have a most important job to do, guiding the development of groups of young miracles. And leaders have an equally important task, empowering staff to do their best and helping them to find gratification in their work.

In the discussion of leaders and staff, readers will often see the expression "working with" but not "working for." This means that leaders coteach with staff, whatever education, certification, and experience staff have. Have you ever seen a "support" staff member who related better to some children and in some situations than the leader? My coteacher would only have to say *eya* or *gaswiin* (Ojibwe for yes and no), and the children would smile or quickly stop. Our *nookomis* (grandmother) was especially friendly with children who were just learning English and spoke Ojibwe at home. They always started out shy with me (a tall white guy with a mustache both below and above his nose). It took time, friendliness, and jokes only a preschooler could appreciate before they would confidently go about their business of learning.

## Staff and Leaders

The staff that leaders work with varies, depending on the job description of the leader. Lead teachers in most early childhood (EC) classrooms work with some combination of

- coteachers;

- assistant teachers;

- education assistants;

- paraprofessionals ("paras");

- classroom aides;

- parent volunteers;

- other volunteers;

- specialists; and

- interns, practicum students, and student teachers.

All of them in a child's view, teachers.

Large programs typically use "multi-classroom" professionals, such as

- classroom managers;

- program coordinators;

- education coordinators;

- staff development facilitators; and

- assistant directors.

> I once supervised student teachers in a small rural community where the lead teacher, Margaret (a former student), was also the director. The fully licensed teacher/director worked with two assistants to provide (1) full-day child care, (2) a morning preschool program, (3) private kindergarten, and (4) after-school care. She balanced the number of slots using Minnesota state guidelines. Later Margaret could have run for mayor—she had the prior experience, and the votes of all her families in her pocket.

These multiclassroom professionals work with lead teachers and often the rest of the staff in the categories above. If there is only one multiclassroom professional, that person is usually the assistant director who provides general assistance to the director.

Directors work with multiclassroom professionals and classroom personnel, along with any clerical, janitorial, and food-service staff. Directors coordinate with outside managerial entities, often that house the program, such as education institutions, nonprofit programs, and host companies. They also coordinate with outside professionals: early childhood special education teachers, therapists of different kinds, and others, such as medical professionals—always with the permission of participating families. Assistant directors help with or take on some of these duties.

Working together, the job of EC leaders and teaching staff is to create and sustain an encouraging early childhood community. The definition at the end of chapter 6 still works:

> An encouraging EC community is a physical and social place where young children, family members, and the professionals who serve them all have acceptance as worthy members of the group. It is a friendly setting for living and learning that includes all. Encouraging EC communities begin within the minds of its leaders.

In everyday terms, an encouraging EC community is a place where folks want to be—even when sick—as opposed to not wanting to be there when they are well. Simple as that.

## Staff Outside of Work

Whatever the staffing arrangement, professionals who lead must manage a mix of relationships with fellow adults to coordinate efforts at creating encouraging EC communities. In this effort, it is easy for leaders to tell themselves that personnel should be making their jobs their top life priority. Although this presumption is unrealistic, even for personnel at high pay levels in other professions, the low incomes of EC personnel totally undercut this notion.

Any setting that a young child is in is a learning setting and hopefully an encouraging community. For this reason, the book does not differentiate between school district preschool programs, private and agency-run preschools, Head Start, child care centers, family child care homes, and any other setting where children are outside of the home.

The 2017 Annual Report of the Children's Defense Fund (sadly) points out, "In 2015, the annual median wage for child care workers was less than that for parking lot attendants in 30 states." Median annual child care worker wages ranged from $18,140 in Mississippi to $25,450 in New York. To cite more statistics from the Defense Fund Report, here are average annual wages in the EC field from four sample states.

| Sample States | Child Care Workers | Head Start Teachers | Preschool Teachers | Kindergarten Teachers | Parking Lot Attendants |
|---|---|---|---|---|---|
| New York | $24,450 | $29,050 | $31,100 | $60,120 | $20,900 |
| Mississippi | $18,140 | $21,842 | $24,970 | $39,800 | $18,670 |
| Minnesota | $22,470 | $28,192 | $32,130 | $53,110 | $21,620 |
| Montana | $19,100 | $19,900 | $25,900 | $44,230 | $20,150 |

With the exception of prekindergarten teachers in some states on school master contracts, EC personnel make very low salaries. If they are the main wage earners in their families, EC workers are close to and often below poverty guidelines. So, like many of the families their programs serve, staff members tend to be members of families beset with income insecurity and adverse experiences.

Early childhood leaders know the reasons for the low incomes. Child care does not receive the tax-funded subsidies that public schools do. Except in the most well-off communities where programs can charge what child care actually costs, EC staff subsidize the cost of care with their low wages. In all likelihood, the reason that preschool teacher salaries are "less low" in the table is that today many preschools are affiliated with school systems. State taxes bolster these salary figures. Early childhood teachers in unsubsidized programs make less.

So, too many staff arrive at their jobs with basic financial insecurities in terms of housing, transportation, food, medical costs, student loan debts, and the list goes on. Staff know firsthand the effects of poverty on their own children—including the heightened danger of unmanageable stress. Leaders who acknowledge the challenges staff face, who are as supportive as they can be of complicated life situations, significantly aid staff members in wanting to come to work and in wanting to join in to build encouraging communities. Leaders cannot ignore the lives outside work that all (including leaders) leave and return to each workday. Listening to staff as worthwhile human beings assists them in getting past personal difficulties when they come through the workplace door.

How do you show the interest that builds relationships? Going back to chapter 3, in their communications with staff members, leaders take the time and make the effort to use

1. contact talks;

2. acknowledge and pause;

3. smiling and nodding;

4. friendly appropriate touch;

5. friendly humor;

6. compliment sandwiches;

7. calming;

8. describe-express-direct; and

9. remembering names, conversations, and promises.

As with children, the harder a staff member is to understand, the more the leader uses guidance communication practices to build and maintain relationships and group spirit. Up to the final point of "it's just not working out," leaders try to use guidance leadership at the "liberation" level with staff having difficult times. (Sorry, I know what I am asking. See the section "Outside Professionals" on page 102.)

## Staff, Especially Men

Staff members of any color and gender who work well with children are a blessing—a gift for the children, their families, and the EC community. Nevertheless, studies cited by MenTeach, among others, indicate that children have an easier time identifying with teachers of the same racial/cultural grouping *and* of the same gender. The ideal for any program is to have a balance of staff that totally reflects our diverse society. The best we can do is recruit proactively and work for team spirit with the staff we hire.

For more than twenty years, MenTeach has been a leading group worldwide advocating for diverse male teachers. For more information about references in this section, go to www MenTeach .org/resources. The news release below is accessible at www .bizjournals.com/ twincities /prnewswire/press_releases /Minnesota/2018/12/18.

MINNEAPOLIS, Dec. 18, 2018 /PRNewswire/—MenTeach has announced that for the first time in United States history, the percentage of men working in child care has increased to 6.3%. (U.S. Bureau of Labor Statistics.) In a study out of Harvard University, 97.9% of survey participants in the education field "strongly agree" or "agree": It's important for men to work with young children. The data further showed that there were three primary reasons men did not enter nor remain in the profession: (1) Stereotypes—some believe that men aren't capable of caring for young children; (2) Fear of false accusations—men worry they may be falsely accused of harming children; (3) Low status and low pay—like many predominantly female professions, child care can be low pay and status.

Despite these challenges, more men work with young children, reflecting some interesting changes in the last several years that may be influencing this upward trend.

Still a long way to go, but with men teachers among the teaching staff, girls and boys have an increased number of male role models in their lives. For some children, male teachers might be the only role models they can build secure attachments with. Male teachers working alongside female teachers make the EC community richer. The nurturing styles, behavior-management practices, and teaching approaches of men in EC add a dimension to programming that the Harvard study indicates has wide parental acceptance. Let's discuss the three identified challenges men face in entering and remaining in early childhood care and education.

**1. Overcoming Stereotypes:** Many male teachers grew up in families with parents who were teachers themselves. For these guys, teaching kids is no big deal. Other families were just plain super-nurturing. Nurturing young children became natural for these guys, possibly starting with brothers and sisters. Boys who helped out with parents that were family child care providers have an especially easy time thinking of themselves as EC teachers, a major role model having done the job before their eyes for their entire lives.

Over my years of teaching early childhood education (ECE) at Bemidji State University in Minnesota, I was always pleased when we had men as well as women in our classes. Two guys especially stand out, a former sheriff's deputy and a football player. Before student teacher placements, wary cooperating teachers conducted interviews with both, then quickly became impressed with their guy student teachers. Male teachers with young children tend to feel comfortable with who they are. These young men always have impressed me for their individual strength in going beyond the stereotypes. And there are more out there who just need recruitment, opportunity, and support.

**2. Fear of False Accusations:** Transparent policies and practices can alleviate these concerns for all staff, especially men. Program booklets, gone over with new staff and families alike, are important. Among other topics, the booklets should address "touch" policies with suggestions like these:

- Friendly appropriate touch is a nurturing tool that all staff, women and men, use with young children.

- There are times when touch is essential, ranging from changing "nappies," potty business, and wetting accidents, to helping very young children get outdoor clothes on and off. These tasks are performed whenever needed by both men and women.

- There are times when children need nurturing touch, like a hug or to sit on a lap. Parents and staff should discuss at an early point parents' comfort levels regarding nurturing touch, with the understanding that the agreed-to practices for families will be used by women and men caregivers alike.

- Whenever possible, more than one staff member is to be present when a caregiver uses essential and nurturing touch.

- When emergencies come up, staff need to use touch alone with a child. They should announce and/or report this occurrence to other adults.

- An "open-door" policy that invites and welcomes parent volunteers into classrooms (after any necessary background checks) is reassuring for families.

Practices are as important as policies. Leaders need to guide staff to work as a team and trust each other. Training and communication exercises for "pods" of staff are important in building mutual respect and team spirit. In the event that a parent interprets a comment by a child to mean an inappropriate action might have occurred, there should always be a review of the circumstances. Such reviews typically should be headed by an "out of classroom" leader. If fellow staff know and trust a team member who is male, the likelihood is much less that a mistaken complaint will go far.

On the other hand, any staff member, man or woman, who finds it difficult to build solid work relationships and gain acceptance as a team member will face a "false accusation" basically alone. The isolated staff member is at risk for dire consequences. From the beginning, the role and responsibility of the leader is to build a closely working team.

**3. Low Status and Low Pay:** Men who go into the EC field know the job is important even if in the eyes of many the job status is low. The low pay is a real problem, though, for men as it is for women. In fact, the biggest challenges leaders might face with staff relate directly and indirectly to pay issues.

Mason graduated with a degree in elementary education and additional licensure in prekindergarten education. The search committee for a northwest Minnesota Head Start agency (including parents) recommended Mason as their top classroom teacher candidate, and Mason was hired.

After a couple of years of successful classroom teaching, Mason applied for a home visitor position with the same Head Start program. The base for the position was in a community school not far from where he lived. Head Start administration was not sure about their successful male classroom teacher becoming a home visitor, but the parents on the search committee again were enthusiastic. Mason got the position.

As one of the only male home visitors in the state, Mason again made his mark. School district administration in the community noticed this successful leader and saw how well he coordinated with school district prekindergarten and kindergarten teachers. The superintendent offered Mason a kindergarten teaching position. About to get married and start a family, Mason accepted.

A few Head Start folks were angry that Mason "had deserted them." Most recognized Mason's situation and were sad that Head Start could not match school district salaries. Mason confided to me that he loved working for Head Start, but he could not pass up the school district offer that included a much higher salary and full benefits.

When a male teacher joins an EC program, resentments by some staff should be understandable. Female staff might suspect that the guy is just taking the job as an upward career move, either by jumping the line into program administration or "moving up" into an elementary school teaching position. Another possible irritant is the positive attention males receive for their work relative to women, who are "just expected" to perform the same duties.

In building a team that works together, leaders might consider meeting with existing staff regarding new male teachers. Recognizing the increased richness that diversity brings to the community, the leader models and teaches this inclusivity to all. Here is a case where the social smarts of leaders come into play. Leaders endeavor to place new male teachers with teams that will take pride in having a male teacher among their ranks. If placement choices are limited, leaders model and teach this pride. Depending on the attitudes, especially of the veterans, this matter can be difficult but worth working together on to resolve. Leaders recruit proactively and team-build inclusively, even if "Kumbaya" is not the theme song they give to their efforts.

## The Importance of Program Booklets

In my view, program booklets are undervalued and underused in EC education. A strong point of creating and using the booklets is this: they can provide an opportunity for leaders and staff to work out and record what is most important to them in terms of a mission statement, goals, practices, and due process for both parents and staff. I suggest saving everyday matters like attendance and fee policies, schedules, calendars, and weather closure—rubber on the road stuff—for another document, maybe called something like *Policies and Procedures*.

Program booklets and policies and procedures booklets should, of course, be available electronically. But in addition, hardcopies of each should be freely available for new staff, parents, and outside consultants. Leaders emphasize that the booklets should really be used, a practice that leaders need to model. Program booklets—especially if followed—show that the program has its stuff together for all to see.

Below are listed some topics that might be included in program booklets:

- Names and work contact information for leaders and members of the staff: A list of staff names should be included along with their roles. A general statement might explain that staff should be contacted through the director or specified multiclassroom professional. This contact information should be prominently displayed.

- Mission statement for the program: The process of developing the statement is important. A representative committee of the program might develop a draft document. All staff should then have the opportunity to have input. Directors would need to coordinate the statement, and the document itself, with sponsoring agencies—Head Start, Y programs, school districts, companies, and so forth.

- Goals of the program: The goals should follow directly from the mission statement. Maybe four to seven goals is a range worth aiming for.

- Education practices: Hopefully all programs would refer to documents from the National Association for the Education of Young Children and/or agencies such as Head Start that put front and center Developmentally Appropriate Practice.

- Guidance practices: Several sources of information are out there. :-})

- Practices relating to appropriate friendly touch: A sign of the times is that this section needs to be included, but parents want to know about this aspect of care of their children. Keep things transparent.

- Home-school relations: The program should stress that the program desires to build partnerships with all parents. A list of typical practices and activities for building partnerships would be helpful to include. One such activity might be early meetings to go over the program booklet with parents. Another is a clearly stated open-door policy.

- Due process and redress practices: If parents ever have a concern, what steps can they take? If they don't feel their concern is alleviated, what agencies can parents contact?

## Outside Professionals

EC programs are communities within communities. Building bridges early with outside entities that might have connections with the program is proactive leadership. The matter of professional consultants who observe, assess, and provide concentrated services for individual children, though, is understandably tricky. It (almost) goes without saying that outside professionals are consulted in relation to individual children *only* with family permission. Further, program professionals should be familiar with consultants and be confident that they will respond sensitively to parents, be respectful, and not patronize or judge them or their children.

Before any referrals, staff build relationships with families. Only when parents reach engagement Level 2: Active Educational Engagement with One's Child (chapter 6) are they likely to accept advisement about a specialist working with their child. Before a parent-teacher partnership is forged, parents are likely to feel that such a recommendation is a judgment about their parenting. Perhaps based on their personal experiences, visions of "my child needs special education; I must be doing something wrong" slog through their brains.

A request to have a specialist observe a child should never be a surprise to parents—just as recommendations on any big issues should not be. Teachers who observe atypical behaviors and physical characteristics should keep dated notes and records and discuss the possibility with fellow staff. When something outside of usual developmental expectations is established as possible, leaders take the concern to parents as soon as possible.

How EC professionals approach parents is crucial. They have to gauge how parents are progressing toward Level 2 and share the information sensitively so as not to disrupt the progress. They always convey their perceptions during an in-person conference. In meeting with parents, leaders should follow the three-phase procedure discussed in chapter 6. Before a meeting, leaders might even work out a multilayer compliment sandwich for how to word the matter with parents.

If it seems like parents are not ready to accept a referral for an outside professional to work with their child, leaders accept the viewpoint and say they will continue to give feedback on the matter to them. Parents need to know whether the issue is getting better, worse, or staying the same.

## Who Are These Professionals?

All states have mandated systems for screening, assessment, and treatment of atypical conditions. Two starting points are usually EC special education programs attached to school systems and local Head Start programs. Early childhood special education (ECSE) teachers are among the outside professionals that program leaders should get to know before any referral is even thought of. One approach is to visit the professionals at *their* place of work, get acquainted, and give them a copy of your program booklet. This is true for Head Start as well, although Head Start is available only in some communities. Head Start serves children with disabilities from families of any income level and often partners with ECSE in diagnostic and remediation procedures. Working with parents, EC leaders need to be proactive in lining up these no-cost services.

Titled "Comprehensive Guidance," the vignette first appeared in a Guidance Matters column back in 2008. The vignette provides a model for how child care teacher Robin Bakken pulled together all resources available in a comprehensive effort to assist a single mom and her child. Still my go-to handout in training sessions, it provides a clear example of liberation teaching with a child and his parent.

As well, program leaders network with outside professionals in regard to lesser-known resources in the community. Other lesser-used resources might include medical professionals, family and child therapists, specialists from nonprofit groups, and individual social services personnel whom the leaders know work well with the types of families served by the program. Early childhood professionals use friendly, persistent leadership in these efforts, as Robin Bakken did in this often-cited vignette.

I met Joe and his mother, Becky, at a Getting to Know You conference before school started. Joe seemed to be a curious, typical 2½-year-old. His mother was young and a full-time college student. I could tell immediately that Becky truly loved her son, and she appeared to be a good caregiver.

Two weeks into the program, Joe began to have trouble getting along with other children. His anxiety level, beginning at drop-off time, seemed to be high. When his personal space was "invaded," often during group activities, Joe responded by pulling children's hair, kicking, or yelling, "Shut up!" When teachers intervened, Joe cried and kicked them. After a few weeks of attempting to guide Joe to use kind words and gentle touches, the director, other staff members, and I decided we needed to pursue a more comprehensive approach.

I began holding short weekly conferences with Becky to get to know her better and to offer her encouragement in her parenting. One day shortly after our meeting, I happened to look out the window and notice Becky sitting on the steps, crying. I took my break early and went out to talk with her. Becky shared her frustration over Joe's behavior: "Why does he act this way? I am tired and don't understand. He is so naughty!"

I responded, "Joe is a very sweet and special boy, and his behavior is the way he responds to stress. He feels threatened by many things right now, and he reacts in the only way he knows. It is mistaken behavior, and it is our job to guide him. It isn't an easy job." I reached over and gave her a hug.

My relationship with Becky continued to grow, and so did her trust in me. Together with other staff members and the director, we developed an individual guidance plan for Joe. At one conference, Becky suggested that we implement a reward system. We tried a sticker chart that recorded and rewarded hourly progress—until Joe lost interest.

Becky and I decided that we would call her any time three serious conflicts occurred in a day. When Joe and I called, I first explained the situation to Becky and then had Joe talk with her. Becky was firm but loving. Joe loved talking with his mother, and we would generally see a more relaxed Joe after these phone calls. (I kept tabs to make sure the calls didn't become a "habit.")

Joe's conflicts with other children continued, and he needed someone nearby at all times to direct him to more appropriate behavior. I would calm Joe by holding and rocking him. Sometimes I sang. After Joe was calm, I used guidance talks, and he talked to me about what happened. These interactions encouraged bonding and a feeling of trust between us.

I also used humor. I gave Joe options of words to use when he was upset. Yelling "Pickle!" became a favorite. I also gave Joe a cushy ball to hold during stressful situations such as circle time and made sure that a student teacher or I sat next to him. We rubbed Joe's back or arm or held him on our laps. The ball kept his hands busy and the touch calmed him.

Drop-off time was difficult for Joe and set the mood for the day. With the director's assistance, I arranged to meet Joe in the office or lounge to spend one-on-one time with him, playing a game or reading. The other staff noticed the difference in Joe—and the entire group—on the days I helped ease him into the class.

Eventually Becky agreed with the staff that an outside mental health assessment was needed for Joe's behavior. Dealing with people outside our center made Becky uncomfortable. To ease her stress, I stayed involved during the assessment process. I worked with the director and others to find resources for Becky; these included a family play therapy program and the school district's early childhood family education classes for young parents. To keep up communication, the teaching staff who worked the later shift talked daily with Becky, and I left happy grams. (Happy grams are brief, positive notes about the child and his or her behavior.) Robin left the notes for the later shift staff to give to Becky, to supplement their own comments to her. Throughout this whole time, the director was a great support to me—and to Becky too.

One day four months into working with Joe, he was building with Duplos when a classmate sat down next to him and took a Duplo off Joe's tower. Joe's previous response would have been to pull the child's hair. This time, however, he shouted, "NO, thank you!" We were so proud of Joe for using his words.

Our guidance plan was finally showing success. Joe learned to say what he needed and what he didn't like. Baby steps were all we needed. Joe grew and so did we.

## Venting and Staff Support

Given the stressors and challenges of the work, all personnel need sources of support, people they can vent to and not be judged by. It helps greatly to have teammates at work whom individuals can lean on. I remember two kindergarten teachers (one a former student) who would arrive early so they could drink coffee together and on occasion go for a walk outside—even during winter in northern Minnesota! The two talked about children in their groups, the administration's many decisions, and family matters, sometimes flat out venting, but the talks always stayed between the two. Sometimes venting has to happen; just keep it confidential. This is the hallmark of being professional.

At a large child care center in the basement of a church, one preschooler, Robby, was driving staff bonkers. On a daily basis, he fell into and caused more conflicts than the rest of the group combined. Five experienced graduate students were assigned by our professor to offer support and consultation services to "City Child Care." One of our team members, Zoey, had built a great rapport with a member of the staff. She confided to Zoey that Robby and some staff had a mutual *non*admiration thing going on (a personality conflict) that this staff member thought was detrimental.

The grad students were holding a series of snack-fueled meetings after the kids left—the staff was getting workshop credit, so they all attended. The grad students explained the value of venting, with "what people say here stays here" being the condition. We asked them if sometimes one child or another might give them problems. Holy tomoley, did many in the group let loose about Robby!

We let them vent and then asked them to share positive points about the child and his behavior. After one adult said, "He is gone sometimes," other staff more sympathetic to the child spoke up. We explained the importance of sometimes letting our frustrations out, and all of us agreed we would look for positives in the fifty-two-month-old.

The next week at our meeting, there was general agreement about how much Robby had improved! (Or, how much the attitudes of the staff had!) We grad students were amazed. We then talked with the staff team about doing more activities with the children in small family groups. We suggested that some children might be grouped with teachers who got along with those children well. The program's assistant director set up the groups using this strategy. In his small family group with a teacher who cared about him, Robby's behavior really did improve. We grad students were happy camp counselors.

Given both the complications of life and the challenges of the job, all EC workers need the outside support of family members and friends. You can unload to pets, but you have to watch your tone of voice. With supportive people outside of work whom you trust, you can let it all go. Just if you do it a lot, get them an occasional bottle of wine, dinner out, favorite box of tea, or a twelve-pack to let them know how much they mean to you. (And be sure to listen back.) Considering the alternative—and with the usual cautions about privacy—venting really helps. Just pick your confidant wisely.

One other word about support for *you*. Connections with others outside of work help keep leaders grounded, such as with faith communities, sports leagues, meditation activities, physical fitness centers (going with a friend is good), and clubs and groups that share your interests. Try to find the time.

And, it is a sign of strength not weakness to locate professional help for yourself. (In some locations, employee assistance programs—EAPs—offer such counseling at no or little cost.) Life is great, but there is just so much of it! You have a lot put on your shoulders, including what this retired professor, sitting in an easy chair drinking probably coffee, has put on you. Do it, but only for yourself when you are ready. "It's okay. It might help you feel better."

## The Teaching Team Model

The model for staff relations that empowers encouraging learning communities is the differentiated staffing teaching team model (TTM). A more traditional model is used primarily in K–12 schools, the teacher-paraprofessional model—where the teacher "teaches" and the para "assists." This model has a hierarchy, in large part due to trends in contract negotiations between K–12 teachers and administrations over the years. In my view, to elevate the professional status of teachers, contract negotiations have resulted in clear distinctions between professionals "prepared to be teachers" and usually (but not always) lesser-educated paraprofessionals, "paras."

So, teachers read books to the whole group while paras prepare tables for snack or lunch. Teachers take children to an activity room, while paras stay behind to tend to children who have wet their pants or can't find their sneakers.

In EC communities, the teaching team model is a better fit. The TTM is more collegial and socially responsive than having a teacher "in charge" with an assistant who is performing a role close to that of a servant. First of all, the children see a real team, adults of different backgrounds and job titles who plan and work together. Cooperation is what a democracy is about, in my view totally preferred over a system that models social stratification and adults "deserving" of different levels of respect. In the guidance approach, encouraging classrooms do have definite leaders but leaders who model a democratic rather than an authoritarian approach.

Staff feel elevated under TTM and are likely to experience more job gratification. The close relationship between being accepted as a contributing team member and job gratification is what TTM is about. Remember the five democratic life skills? They pertain to all of us, including staff, and not just children:

1. Find acceptance as a member of the group and as a worthy individual.

2. Express strong emotions in nonhurting ways.

3. Solve problems creatively, by oneself and with others.

4. Accept unique human qualities in others.

5. Think intelligently and ethically.

Hopefully, proactive recruiting results in a staff that is beyond DLS 1 and 2 and is meeting DLS 3, 4, and 5. Anyone can have adverse experiences, though. In TTM, staff tend to be there to listen and pick each other up. When EC teachers (inclusive definition) themselves know they are making progress with DLS, they will model and teach these skills with the children they share their lives with, every time all walk through the door. We are going for happy campers and happy camp counselors *both* in the EC learning community.

# Wrap-Up

Early childhood professionals mold human beings like teachers at no other level. You, as much as any social force, are helping our society make it to the twenty-second century. Leaders and staff that work as a close team are in the best position to guide children to gain the democratic life skills from which society as a whole benefits. Let's keep working to enable others outside of the EC learning community to recognize this truth. I dearly hope you have accomplished quite a bit of significant learning through this book. The three-hour exam on its contents has been canceled. Go forth and teach good.

**Take-away question:** In what ways do the five democratic life skills pertain to both young children and the EC professionals who work with them? What are some of the similarities and differences between the two groups in using the theory?

## Reference Notes

Children's Defense Fund. 2017. *The State of America's Children, 2017.* www.childrensdefense .org.

Gartrell, Dan. 2008. "Comprehensive Guidance." Guidance Matters column in *Young Children*, December 2008. National Association for the Education of Young Children.

———. 2012. *Education for a Democratic Society. How Guidance Teaches Young Children Democratic Life Skills.* Washington, DC: NAEYC.

———. 2013. *A Guidance Approach for the Encouraging Classroom*, 6th ed. Boston: Cengage Learning.

Loewenberg, A. 2017. "There's a Stigma around Men Teaching Young Kids: Here's How We Can Change It." October 19. MenTeach.org. www. menteach.org/pages/blogarticles /index.html.

# Index

psychological growth
as motivational source for behavior, 17–18
skills based on
acceptance of unique human qualities of
others, 23–24
problems solved creatively, 21–23
psychological safety
as motivational source for behavior, 17–18
skills based on
expressing strong emotions in nonhurting
ways, 20–21
finding acceptance as member of group
and as worthy individual, 20
public embarrassment
as prevalent form of punishment, 21, 54
techniques for avoiding, 21, 54, 70
punishment
alternatives to, in guidance, 6
brain development and, 70
bully-victim dynamic and, 6
group, 51
increases difficulty of "emotional-social"
development, 6
as part of conventional discipline, 5, 6, 14
public embarrassment as most prevalent form of,
21, 54, 70
stress levels elevated by, 11, 14

race and poverty, 83
reactive aggression, 45, 51, 61
readiness
described, 65
developmentally appropriate practice as pathway
to, 65
families and, 71
as state of mind, 66
teaching practices to support, 73
1. acknowledgment and pause. *See*
acknowledgment and pause (AAP)
2. daily contact talks with each child, 30,
68–69
3. accommodating early reasoning skills,
69
4. firm but friendly ways of teaching, 70
5. using developmentally appropriate
practices with every child, 70–71
6. building partnerships with families,
71–73
reasoning skills. *See* executive function
recall, in executive function, 8
reflective listening, 32, 85
relationships
aggression and, 46
building
with families, 71–73, 86–90, 103
guidance and, 29
secure, outside of conflict situations, 14
*See also* communication practices
calming ability and, 70
with children without democratic life skill #1, 20

importance of trust, 12, 27
making every child feel welcomed and valued,
47–48
model for staff, 107–108
readiness and secure, 65, 66
with staff, 96–97
with surrogate parents, 75–76
using compliments to start, 67
remembering names, conversations, and promises,
41–42
"restoring order" compared to de-escalation, 52
Rogers, Carl, 1

same-sex parent families, 77
self-protection
amygdala and, 7
mistaken behavior and, 61
shaming, 11
significant learning
child's positivity about learning experience, 66
guidance encourages, 1
stays with and changes child, 63
sign language, 79
single-parent families, 76, 77
smiling and nodding, 32, 33–34
social awareness development and executive
function, 8
socially influenced mistaken behavior, 12–13
staff
input for mission statement and program
booklets, 102
leaders and
empowering all, 93
importance of working closely as team,
99–100, 101, 106–108, 109
pay issues with, 100–101
supportive of, 96
members of, 93–95
men as
fear of false accusations, 99–100
importance of, in early childhood
community, 97–98
low status and pay, 100–101
overcoming stereotypes of, 98–99
model for relationships among, 107 108
outside of work, 95–96
stressors on, and venting, 106–107
as teachers, 93–94
training about touching, 99
wages, 95–96
stereotypes, as part of lessons, 63–64
stress
behaviors and, 7–8, 9
healthy, 9
levels of mistaken behavior and, 13
punishment elevates levels of, 11, 14
reactive aggression and, 45
repression of children's ideas and, 66
on staff and venting, 106–107
trust-based relationships and dealing with, 27

types of, 8–9
unmanageable (toxic)
    adverse experiences and, 66
    causes of, 8
    conflict and, 9, 11
    described, 9
    strong unmet needs mistaken behavior and, 12
    struggle to meet democratic life skills #1 and #2, 27
stress/act-out syndrome
    described, 11
    effects of, 12
strong unmet needs mistaken behavior, 13
"The Superior Social Skills of Bilinguals" (Kinzler), 81
surrogate parents, 75–76
swear words, 37–38

task persistence, in executive function, 8
task talks, 30
teachers
    defining, 1
    early childhood special education, 103
    as learners, 84
    team model, 107–108
    *See also* leaders; staff
Teaching Team Model (TTM), 107–108
thinking skills, building, by using acknowledgment and pause, 67
time-out versus cooling-down time, 39
touching. *See* friendly appropriate touch
touch policies, 34–35
toxic stress. *See* unmanageable stress
Treuer, Anton, 79

understanding, as mindful choice, 10
unmanageable stress
    adverse experiences and, 66
    causes of, 8
    conflict and, 9, 11
    described, 9
    strong unmet needs mistaken behavior and, 12
    struggle to meet democratic life skills #1 and #2, 27

violence and Adverse Childhood Experiences, 12

Weber, Nancy, 9, 10
"Welcoming and Supporting Dual Language Learners" (NAEYC website), 82
whole-group meetings
    examples of topics covered, 49, 50
    group punishment compared to, 51
    guidelines for, 49
    leader's role, 50
worthiness of individual, 20